The Welcoming Classroom

Building Strong Home-to-School Connections for Early Learning

JOHNNA DARRAGH ERNST, PHD

DEDICATION

To John, Alex, and Megan

ACKNOWLEDGMENTS

I'd like to thank Stephanie Roselli for her solicitation of the manuscript and her assistance in its development. Thanks, as always, to the staff of the Heartland Child Development Lab for providing wonderful applied examples. In particular, I would like to thank Joellen Scott for her contributions and Jane Schall and John Ernst for their practical assistance and ongoing support.

BULK PURCHASE

DISCLAIMER

GH10124
A Gryphon House Book

THE

Building Strong Home-to-School Connections for Early Learning

Welcoming
CLASSROOM

Johnna Darragh Ernst, PhD

GRYPHON HOUSE, INC
Lewisville, NC

COPYRIGHT

Published by Gryphon House, Inc.
P. O. Box 10, Lewisville, NC 27023
800.638.0928; 877.638.7576 (fax)
Visit us on the web at www.gryphonhouse.com.

Cover photographs courtesy of Stephanie Whitfrield, taken at The Creative Center for Childhood Research and Training, Tallahassee, FL. Interior photographs courtesy of Shutterstock.com © 2014.

LIBRARY OF CONGRESS CATALOGING-IN-PUBLICATION DATA

Ernst, Johnna Darragh.
  The welcoming classroom : building strong home-to-school connections for early learning / Johnna Darragh Ernst, PhD.
       pages cm
  Includes bibliographical references and index.
   ISBN 978-0-87659-482-7
  1. Early childhood education--Parent participation--United States. 2. Parent-teacher relationships--United States. 3. Communication in education--United States. 4. Community and school--United States. 5. Home and school--United States. 6. School children--Family relationships--United States. I. Title.
   LB1139.35.P37E65 2013
   371.21--dc23
                                    2014001297

Table of Contents

Preface

My decision to write this book was inspired by personal and professional experiences. I have found that working with families can be both incredibly rewarding and challenging. On one hand, there is widespread recognition that family engagement is central to supporting children's success, and there is great reward in building thriving partnerships with families. On the other hand, challenges often arise regarding how to successfully engage families. These challenges can become particularly marked when practitioners and families have differing perspectives.

Successfully engaging families requires understanding what each of us brings to interactions with family members. Before we can form successful partnerships, we must fully understand the unique lens that we see the world through, including our own individual schemas, biases, and ways of interacting with those around us. This book includes a strong focus on understanding our unique social identities and the richness and complexities of diverse family identities. This understanding is essential to effective communication and collaboration. I examine fundamental communication and collaboration skills and discuss their meaning within the larger context of culturally competent communication. The goal of communication and collaboration is developing respectful, reciprocal, responsive relationships, programs, and environments.

Engaged families make an incredible difference in the lives of their children. Successfully engaging families requires adopting a strengths-based approach, in which professionals recognize family strengths, priorities, concerns, resources, and dreams and work collaboratively with families to support children's success.

Your Role in Engaging Families

CHAPTER 1

Every day, you make an incredible difference in the lives of young children. Your daily, respectful, responsive interactions; intentional teaching strategies; and applications of developmentally appropriate practices assure that you support the development and learning of each child in your class. Your work with families is incredibly important as well. As the family is the child's first and most important teacher, the partnerships you establish with families can affect the family and child in the short term and—in a wonderful, rippling effect—for many years to come.

You can make an important, lasting difference in the lives of young children by fully engaging families within the early childhood community. Engagement means that families can access all the early childhood community has to offer and can meaningfully participate in the classroom and program. Family engagement supports children's success based on a dynamic, interactive process that includes the following:

a shared responsibility among families, communities, schools, and organizations where families are committed to a child's success;

enduring, continuous commitment across the child's life in which the family's role changes as the child matures into young adulthood;

reinforcement of learning across the multiple contexts in which children learn and develop (Weiss and Lopez, 2009).

Your ability to engage families begins with knowing yourself. Who are you as a communicator? What are your social identities and cultural framework? How do these factors interact with the social identities and cultural frameworks of families in your classroom and influence your ability to form effective partnerships with families? What strategies are most effective in engaging each family within your larger organization and classroom? Your knowledge and skills as a culturally competent communicator who works to develop respectful, reciprocal, responsive relationships and environments are essential in ensuring engagement.

Building Strong Foundations

Mutual respect, reciprocity, and responsiveness create the foundation for developing thriving relationships with families (Barerra, Corso, and Macpherson, 2003). Respect recognizes boundaries that define the individual's unique identities. When you respect someone, you are open to her individuality. Reciprocity requires that you provide families an equal voice. While expertise and experience may vary, when there is reciprocity everyone feels validated. Responsiveness allows for taking different directions based on the needs of the individual and the family—responsiveness honors and creates connection and synergy (Barerra, Corso, and Macpherson, 2003).

Building strong foundations that support family engagement requires knowledge and skills, including the following:

communication and collaboration skills and knowledge of how to apply these,

knowledge of your own social identities and cultural framework and how these influence communication and collaboration with others,

culturally competent communication skills,

knowledge of culturally and linguistically competent practices at the organizational level that support each family, and

knowledge of culturally and linguistically competent practices at the classroom level that support each family.

Diversity is shaped by our unique social identities, including such factors as race, gender, age, varied abilities, language, ethnicity, social class, religiosity, the region of the country lived in, political affiliation, and sexuality, including sexual orientation. How we identify with these factors provides us with our cultural framework. The term *culture* is used in this book to refer to the diversity we experience across each of these factors. Successfully engaging each family requires attention to your own social identities and cultural framework, as well as how your identities and framework interact with the families you work with.

Adopting a Strengths-Based Approach

Family engagement supports positive child outcomes. We know, for example, that supporting family engagement improves school readiness, promotes student academic achievement, and increases graduation rates (Henderson and Mapp, 2002). Students with engaged parents throughout early childhood and adolescence are more likely to graduate from high school (Englund, Englund, and Collins, 2008).

We also know that many families experience obstacles that might interfere with their full engagement. A disproportionate number of students who drop out of high school and college are from low-income backgrounds, of racial and ethnic minorities, or have disabilities (Weiss, Lopez, and Rosenberg, 2010). Many of these children and their families are products of a system in which differences are viewed as deficits or are labeled as gaps rather than as potential strengths. When applied to children, the deficit model can be far reaching. The deficit model highlights perceived deficits in children as opposed to seeing each child's wonderful and complex strengths. A child who speaks Spanish and is developing her English skills is on her way to being bilingual; she is not simply deficient in her English proficiency. A child's outstanding math and literacy skills should not be overshadowed by a label that highlights her social challenges. Not only does the deficit model focus on innate challenges, but it also contributes to the overrepresentation of children who are culturally and linguistically diverse in special education (Kalyanpur and Harry, 2012).

When applied to families, the deficit model can be far reaching as well. Consider the Runlez family. They work hard to put food on the table for their children, clothe them, and get them to school each day. In fact, each parent works two jobs because their jobs do not pay a living wage. They may be viewed as people with developing literacy skills who work low-income jobs, or they may be viewed through a lens that highlights their hard work, resilience, and commitment to supporting their children.

Now, let's consider the Mantuez family, who recently emigrated from Mexico. Their preschooler was referred for early intervention services after a series of screening and diagnostic tests. The family has not immediately pursued these services, instead taking time to talk with friends and wait for an upcoming appointment with their family doctor. They may be viewed as responsible people who desire to make a good decision for their child after gaining information from people they trust, or they may be viewed as people who are totally in denial about their child's needs.

Viewing families and children through a positive lens affects the way professionals interact with them. Successfully engaging families requires abandoning the deficit model and learning to adopt a strengths-based approach. The foundation of the strengths-based approach is respect, reciprocity, and responsiveness. This approach leaves no room for an attitude of blame when things go wrong or a lens that highlights perceived shortcomings. This approach adopts a framework of shared responsibility. Families and professionals acknowledge and work within complementary roles to support children's success (Weiss, Lopez, and Rosenberg, 2010). A strengths-based approach views the individual in light of her capacities, talents, competencies, visions, values, and hopes, recognizing that these might be affected by present circumstances, oppression, and trauma (Nissen, 2001). For example, as opposed to looking at the Runlez family's low literacy and low income as risk factors potentially affecting their child's academic success, early childhood professionals can adopt an approach that focuses on the family's desire to support their children's education, their willingness to connect with local resources, and their capacity to apply these supports within their home environment. How people live their lives and the multiple contexts that influence their lives can be a source of support or stress. When adopting a strengths-based approach, the focus becomes maximizing resources to support each individual in her unique situation. The early childhood program, classroom, and professional can be important supports for families.

The strengths-based approach is based on key principles, adapted here to the field of early childhood education:

Every individual, family, group, and community has unique strengths. The role of the professional is to focus on these strengths.

The community and early childhood program is a rich source of resources.

Supports are based on individual priorities.

Collaboration is an essential component of maximizing family strengths.

All people have the inherent capacity to learn, grow, and develop (Saint-Jacques, Turcotte, and Pouliot, 2009).

One of the most important aspects of the strengths-based approach is that it shifts away from an "at-risk" paradigm and moves to one where individuals can overcome challenges when provided with the right supports (Price-Robertson, 2010). The strengths-based approach represents an important shift from "What are families missing?" to "What do families need to develop and thrive?"

You have a critical role in providing supports. Your responsibility includes discovering each family's unique strengths, concerns, priorities, and resources. Once you have

Yesterday, Olga welcomed the Martinez family to her classroom. They recently emigrated from Mexico, are fluent in Spanish, and are developing their English skills. Already part of the classroom community is the Mailloux family, whose children spend the week at their mother's home and the weekend at their father's. The Cappos-Hall family lives with both parents, who work full time for the same company. The Wills family consists of two mothers, and the Lusk family is headed by a single-parent father. The Cazalet family has four children, two of whom are foster children, and one of whom is currently receiving speech and occupational therapy services in Olga's classroom. Just last week, Olga was able to connect the Gaff family with the resources they needed for housing assistance, as the father just lost his job. Olga has not yet met Martin's parents, because his grandmother picks him up every day. These are just a few of the twenty families she interacts with on a daily basis, and each one brings rich diversity to the classroom community and has unique engagement needs.

identified these, you can work closely with each family to develop engagement strategies that enhance their ability to support their child's learning, serve as a partner within the school environment, advocate for their child, and serve as decision makers and leaders. Your work with the family may last a limited period of time, but families who successfully develop these strategies will positively affect their child throughout her school career. Your efforts will ripple out to support the child and family well beyond the time you are directly interacting with them!

Understanding and Defining Families

Close your eyes and picture the typical family. Who is included? Perhaps it looks similar to the family you grew up within, or maybe the family you picture looks like the family of a child in your classroom. Families are incredibly diverse. When you consider the typical family, keep in mind the following thoughts from Laura Howe, shared in her book *The Future of the Family:*

The first thing to remember about the [typical] family is that it doesn't exist. Families exist. All kinds of families in all kinds of economic and marital situations, as all of us can see… The [typical] family? Just which [typical] family did you have in mind? Black or white, large or small, wealthy or poor, or somewhere in between? Did you mean a father-headed, mother-headed, or childless family? First or second time around? Happy or miserable? Your family or mine?

Statistically, like many other countries around the world, the United States is becoming an increasingly globalized nation. According to 2010 U.S. census data, almost half of recent births in the United States are to minorities, with 49.8 percent of infants being members of a race-ethnic minority. More than a quarter of these infants, specifically, are Hispanic, 13.6 percent are African American, and 4.2 percent are Asians (Frey, 2011). Nearly one in two of these children were reported to be of two of more races. Nationally, there is an increasing trend toward gains in a youthful minority population, coupled with a trend toward an aging of the white population.

Currently, the children of immigrants who are also U.S. citizens are the fastest growing component of the child population. These children account for one-fourth of the nation's 75 million children and are projected to make up more than one-third of 100 million U.S. children by 2050 (Tienda and Haskins, 2011). Due to the wave of immigration that has occurred since the 1960s, children have become the most racially and ethnically diverse age group in the United States.

Nearly 15 million children—representing 21 percent of all children in the United States—live in poverty. The current definition of poverty is based on a family income that is below the federal poverty level, defined as $22,350 for a family of four (National Center for Children in Poverty, 2012). Covering basic expenses requires about twice that amount! If that standard is applied, 44 percent of our nation's children live in low-income families. Poverty is identified as the greatest threat to children's overall well-being, as it affects a child's ability to learn and can contribute to social, emotional, and behavioral problems as well as poor health and mental health outcomes (National Center for Children in Poverty, 2012). There are a variety of different factors associated with children's chances of experiencing poverty, including race/ethnicity, parent level of educational attainment, and employment.

ISSUES OF OPPORTUNITY: RACE AND ETHNICITY

Hector and Anya are similar to many children entering kindergarten—they are eager to learn, have parents who want the best for their children, and are looking forward to all the school year has to offer. Both children, however, have experienced obstacles that have interfered with their school readiness: inadequate nutrition in their early years, a lack of access to health care, and poor quality child care. Although their parents are highly motivated to support their success, each child's parents work two jobs and return to homes in unsafe neighborhoods that are short on resources to support their children's development. Hector, Anya, and their families are not alone in experiencing these obstacles, and we know that these obstacles can have far-reaching effects on high-school completion rates, postsecondary education, earnings later in life, and the ability to build assets (Annie E. Casey Foundation, 2006). Hector and Anya need opportunity.

Barriers to opportunity include systemic inequities related to race and ethnicity. African American children score lower on measures of cognitive development when compared to white babies at the age of nine months (Child Trends, 2002). At twenty-four months, this trend has more than tripled, and by age four, the scores of African American children are significantly behind white children in proficiency in letter, number, and shape recognition (Flores, Tomany-Korman, and Olson, 2005).

Hispanic babies are not significantly behind white babies at nine months of age, but by twenty-four months, a gap does develop (Child Trends, 2002). Similar to African American children, there is a significant gap at four years of age. Both Hispanic and African American children arrive in kindergarten and first grade with lower levels of school readiness when compared to white children (Farkas, 2003). These pervasive gaps must be viewed within the context of similar gaps in income, wealth, safety, health, and justice-system involvement.

We know that many risks to development and school readiness are related to low socioeconomic status and that low socioeconomic status is highly connected to race, ethnicity, and other demographic characteristics (Children's Defense Fund, 2012). Many people experience challenges in accessing resources due to language and cultural differences between the provider and the potential user (Annie E. Casey Foundation, 2012). These challenges can be compounded for undocumented and non-English-speaking residents, who are often unaware of services within communities or unable to access these services. Institutionally, families and programs may have varying ideas about child-rearing practices and culturally based ideas about how to prepare a child for success in school. Programs may adopt an attitude of families and children needing to be ready for them, as opposed to adapting program practices to be ready for the diversity of families and children who will come through the doors. Creating opportunity starts with you.

Family diversity encompasses far more than race, ethnicity, or a family's socioeconomic status. Families can also vary by who is included in the family. According to the 2010 U.S. census data, more than half of America's children have spent some time being raised in a single parent family, with a slow and steady rise over the past decade of the number of fathers who are gaining custody of their children (currently four in one hundred). Twenty-five percent of all same-sex households are raising children, and children may be raised by grandparents, other family members, or in foster families. Even when a child is being raised by her biological mother and father, another family member might have the primary decision-making responsibility for the child. To make assumptions about family form and the way the family functions is to potentially miss out on rich opportunities to engage families and form potential partnerships.

It is no surprise that early childhood classrooms are becoming increasingly diverse. Of children with disabilities, 50.9 percent are being served in some type of inclusive early childhood setting (U.S. Department of Education, 2010). The enrollment of dual language learners has increased dramatically in early childhood programs nationwide; this trend is projected to continue (Office of Head Start, 2008). Close to half of the children in early childhood classrooms in the country are from racial or ethnic minorities (Cohn and Bahrampour, 2006). Currently, about 30 percent of children enrolled in Head Start programs are dual language learners, and 85 percent of these children speak Spanish as their primary language (Hernandez, Denton, and McCartney, 2007). These data point to the incredible need for early childhood teachers to be aware of the unique strengths, concerns, priorities, and resources of young children and families. Yet research indicates that most teachers do not receive adequate support to work with diverse populations during their preservice training programs (Winton and McCollum, 2008).

Early childhood professionals must understand who the families within their early childhood community are and must learn what each family needs to be successfully engaged. Each family has a unique history and story, has their own way of acting upon and interacting with the world, and presents opportunities for you to develop mutually rewarding and beneficial connections. It is your responsibility to approach each family to learn who they are and what wonderful mix of strengths they bring to their child's world. From that foundation, you can learn about the family's concerns, priorities, and existing and needed resources, and—within a framework designed to support family engagement—foster a lasting and beneficial partnership.

Meaningfully Engaging Families

Engaging families requires supporting family access and meaningful participation and providing needed supports to both families and professionals. The National Association for the Education of Young Children (NAEYC) and the Division for Early Childhood (DEC) of the Council for Exceptional Children's 2009 joint position statement on early childhood inclusion spells out the factors central to creating high-quality, inclusive environments for young children. The defining features of inclusion also work well when applied to supporting engagement for families:

> All families need access to the early childhood community and the varied activities within it.
>
> Families need individualized supports and accommodations to support their meaningful participation.
>
> Families and teachers need supports in terms of infrastructure and professional development to ensure engagement strategies are developed and implemented.

The environment and the professionals within it need to fluidly respond to each family rather than forcing the family to fit the environment. Create a unique culture based on the children and families served. When you practice reciprocity, you are giving families a voice and input into policies and procedures. Reciprocity implies change and new directions based on shared synergy. While there are some factors in the environment, such as health and safety standards, that are not amenable to change, curriculum, the structure of the day, or communication can change in response to the needs of the classroom and center community. Creating opportunities for input demonstrates your openness and respect to the families within your environment.

Developing this unique culture requires reflection. Carefully consider the range of opportunities and experiences provided for children and families in your program and evaluate potential areas of growth. Table 1.1 offers some professional reflection questions pertaining to access, participation, and supports within early childhood programs and classrooms.

TABLE 1.1: FAMILY ENGAGEMENT REFLECTION QUESTIONS

Family Engagement Variable	Family Engagement Factor Supported	Central Reflection Questions
Program values and validates family participation in decision making related to their child's education.	Access	Do families have meaningful decision-making opportunities that provide for and support their active participation in all aspects of their child's education?
There is a continuous exchange of knowledge and collaboration between families and the early childhood program.	Access	Does the program provide opportunities for families to share unique knowledge by participating meaningfully in volunteer and program events and activities? Do teachers seek information about children and families' lives and the communities they live within? Do they integrate this information into the curriculum and instructional practices in a meaningful way?
Consistent, two-way communication that is respectful of each family's linguistic preferences is facilitated.	Participation	Do both the program and the families initiate timely, continuous, linguistically respectful communication based on conversations about both the individual child and larger program?
The program and families emphasize creating and sustaining learning activities at home and in the community that extend the teachings of the program and enhance each child's development and learning.	Participation	Are there opportunities and supports for families to apply what is learned in school in the home and community environment?
Families value learning and support the program. The program and families collaborate in establishing goals for children both within the home and at school.	Supports	Are meaningful goals created for children that reflect family strengths, concerns, and priorities, as well as maximize their resources?
Program leadership and teachers work to create an ongoing and comprehensive system for promoting family engagement through dedication, training, and acquiring needed supports.	Supports	Does program staff have the needed supports to implement family engagement strategies in a comprehensive and systematic way?
(Adapted from Halgunseth et al., 2009.)		

As Table 1.1 implies, although there are defined family engagement factors, support for each family's access and participation is unique, as what each family brings to the early childhood community is unique. Each family will have unique strengths, priorities, concerns, and resources relative to enhancing the development of their child. Identify each family's strengths, priorities, concerns, and resources by asking questions such as the following:

What are the interests, needs, and strengths that could link the child and family with a wider network of supports?

What are the family's current strengths in managing their daily lives and meeting their child's needs? How can these strengths be expanded?

What would the family like to do to support their child's development and learning?

What is the family's approach to problem solving?

What are the family's concerns, hopes, and plans?

(Adapted from Turnbull and Summers, 1987.)

A family strength might be their investment and participation in your preschool program— they bring their child to school regularly and always want to know how their child is doing. You, in turn, support the family's full participation through soliciting their input into curriculum decision making. Because of this reciprocity and your respectful communication, you learn that they want to support their child's developing reading skills. The family is concerned, however, about their ability to accomplish this goal due to their own developing literacy skills. You respond by providing books for the family in both English and their home language, and you coordinate your efforts with the English-as-a-second-language program the family is participating in. You also respond by connecting the family with additional resources in the community, including the local library. Your program director makes sure that you and your coteacher are able to attend professional development workshops on supporting a child and family in developing their English skills while preserving their home language.

Successful collaboration with this family is based on the foundation that you built from respectful, reciprocal, responsive communication and collaboration. We will explore communication and collaboration strategies designed to engage families in a comprehensive, systematic way.

Shaping Family Engagement

Each family who comes to your early childhood community presents a natural opportunity for connection and relationship around a shared interest—their child. To truly respond to families, our understanding of the families and responsiveness to them must be genuine and deep.

Understanding families happens on three different levels, what Kalyanpur and Harry (2012) describe as overt, covert, and subtle levels of cultural awareness. On the overt level, a teacher might recognize a family's concern over a lack of transportation, and she might respond by planning a family event that includes transportation to and from the event. Another teacher might know that a child speaks French at home, and so he might learn a few words of the language and arrange to have a translator for the family during conferences.

We are less likely to be aware of cultural factors at the covert level, as these factors go a bit deeper and are generally not recognized by outward signs. Factors at the covert level of cultural awareness include status (how the role of the teacher is viewed, for example, or how the family members view their role as parent within the early childhood community) or communication styles (such as preferences for greetings, eye contact, or body posture). A family might, for example, not participate in classroom activities and events because they see education as entirely the role of the teacher. Another family might not participate because they feel they have nothing to contribute. One family might view a handshake as disrespectful, and another might feel looking the teacher directly in the eye is disrespectful.

Even less likely to receive our attention are subtle levels of cultural recognition, including recognizing the embedded values and beliefs that underlie people's actions (such as parenting values and how these shape goals for children's behavior). These embedded values and beliefs are often taken for granted and assumed to be universal but are specific to the individual's own culture. A family might value their child's quiet, reserved behavior, for example, and might not respond to or understand your concerns about what you see as the child's lack of interaction with other children. Early childhood professionals must respond at overt, covert, and subtle levels to support connection and engagement with families.

Family engagement strategies need to be comprehensive and systematic. Efforts to engage families are often piecemeal and an add-on to the daily operations of programs and schools rather than integral aspects interwoven into program operations. A classroom might have certain opportunities for communication and collaboration in place—daily conversations and notes home, a family night, opportunities to observe— but the program lacks systemic, integrated, and sustained efforts that are meaningful at all levels of program operations. When efforts are systematic, integrated, and sustained, families not only know what is happening in the classroom but also have input. Families not only know of program events, but also they have helped plan and evaluate them. Families not only benefit from program policies, but also they have helped shape them. Family engagement strategies must be an important part of program structures and processes and must reflect and support family and child goals (Weiss, Lopez, and Rosenberg, 2010).

Understanding the Effects of Family Engagement

Engaging families might sound like a good thing to do—it makes sense that you would want to involve families with each aspect of your early childhood education program. However, research has shown that engaging families has far greater implications than a good feeling that comes from families participating in your program. Engaged families make a difference in the lives of their children! Supporting family engagement improves school readiness, promotes student academic achievement, and increases graduation rates (Henderson and Mapp, 2002). We know that engaged families have children who perform well in school (Izzo et al., 1999) and are more likely to be promoted to the next grade (Mantizicopoulos, 2003). We know that children with engaged families have more positive engagement with peers and other adults and tend to have more positive attitudes overall toward their learning (McWayne et al., 2004). Family engagement also serves as an important buffer, reducing the negative impact of poverty on children's academic and behavioral outcomes. Further, we know that the benefits of family engagement persist over time (Harvard Family Research Project, 2006). The knowledge, skills, and energy you put forth to engage a family now can be a benefit that supports families for many years in the future.

Each family you work with shapes how program outcomes are implemented. The Head Start Parent, Family, and Community Engagement Framework offers seven outcomes to family engagement that programs should strive for:

> supporting family well-being through support for family safety, health, and financial security;
>
> supporting positive parent-child relationships through building warm relationships that nurture children's learning and development;
>
> supporting families as lifelong educators by supporting families in enhancing their child's everyday development and learning at home, in school, and in their communities;
>
> supporting families as learners by supporting families in advancing their own learning interests through education and training that holistically addresses their learning goals, including parenting, careers, and life goals;
>
> supporting family engagement in transitions by supporting families in advocating for their child as they transition to new learning environments throughout the child's educational career;
>
> supporting families' connections to peers and the community through supporting connections to peers and mentors in formal and informal social networks serving to enhance the families' social well-being and community life;
>
> supporting families as advocates and leaders through supporting family participation in leading, decision-making activities, policy development, and other state and local organizing activities to improve their child's learning and development.

These outcomes speak to supporting the family in the present and in the long term, reflecting the idea that the effect you have on a family now can ripple out and affect them for many years to come.

Chapter Reflection Questions

What are your current goals for engaging families within your classroom and program?

What do you see as the greatest benefits to family engagement?

What are some of the strengths of the families you work with on a daily basis?

What do you see as a benefit of viewing families through a lens that focuses on their strengths?

What is your definition of meaningful family engagement?

Questions to Explore with Families

What are your goals for becoming involved in the classroom and program?

What do you see as benefits to becoming involved in your child's education?

What do you feel are some of your family's strengths?

What would a program and classroom that places a priority on engaging families look like?

Foundational Communication and Collaboration Skills

CHAPTER 2

Myra began the day feeling refreshed and ready to face whatever challenges came her way. The previous day, she and her coworkers had attended a workshop on communication and collaboration skills, and Myra was eager to put all that she had learned into practice.

Her first challenge was speaking with Alisha's mother about her concerns regarding Alisha's development. The five-year-old rarely seemed to seek out the company of other children in the classroom and did not seem to respond to other children's bids for play. At morning drop-off, Myra said, "I've been wanting to talk to you about Alisha's interactions with other children." Alisha's mom looked over her shoulder at the clock on the wall. Myra then said, "If now isn't a good time to talk, we can touch base later." Alisha's mom responded, "Right, just drop me a note, and we can figure something out," then hurried off. Her first exchange of the day left Myra feeling brushed off and unheard.

The day did not get much better when, at lunch, another parent expressed concerns he had about his daughter not learning enough math skills in Myra's classroom. Myra thought she had resolved this issue with him previously by explaining how children acquire academic skills, including important basic math skills, through play and guided interactions. As he talked, Myra remembered that she needed to send Alisha's mother a note to set up a conference time and that she also needed to touch base with her director about requesting time off next month. Myra felt like she was keeping up with the conversation by nodding at appropriate times and adding the occasional "I see where you are coming from," and "Uh-huh." She was quite startled when the parent asked, "Are you listening to me?"

Myra's day ended with one of the children in the class being picked up by his grandmother. Her previous exchanges with the grandmother rarely seemed to go well. Today, she walked into the classroom to pick up *her grandson and commented to Myra, "I see he is messy again." Myra did not respond, as she felt that the grandmother was never going to be happy with anything she did.*

As Myra willed the day to end, she wondered what had happened to her enthusiasm to apply her newly learned communication and collaboration skills. She felt misunderstood and not fully able to understand and respond to the concerns of others. Why did she find communication and collaboration to be so challenging?

Defining Communication and Collaboration

Our days are filled with communication! We send messages, receive them, and hope that we understand others while wanting to be understood. Communication plays an essential role in supporting family engagement; it is a tool that enables you to build relationships. Collaboration—based on partnership, shared priorities, and mutually agreed-upon goals—creates rich relationships that support positive outcomes for families, children, and teachers. Effective communication and collaboration are not always easy—they require focus, patience, energy, and skill.

We begin communicating from the time we first draw breath. From that point on, how we communicate becomes increasingly complex and is based on our ability to convey and understand messages in the world around us. These messages are provided in a variety of ways—they might be written, spoken, or nonverbal. Our capacity to miscommunicate, to fail to successfully convey our own message or understand the messages being conveyed to us, is equally complex.

We each have a great capacity to improve our communication skills, and reflection plays a key role in this capacity. In the course of a day, you might have an exchange with a family member in your program that you feel went spectacularly well—your message was clearly conveyed, and you feel that message was received and responded to. On that same day, you might have another exchange with a family member that you felt went poorly—you just could not find the words to clearly express what you were trying to say, and you could sense the person's frustration in understanding your ideas. Reflecting on

APPLYING COMMUNICATION AND COLLABORATION SKILLS:
REFLECTING ON AN EXCHANGE

Select a communication exchange with a family member or coworker in your program.
Reflect on your contributions to the exchange. How did you communicate your message? Think
about what you said, how you positioned your body, your facial expressions (as far as you know),
and your tone of voice.

Consider the outcome. How do feel your communication style contributed to the outcome? What
changes in your style might have produced a different outcome?

Based on your analysis, what parts of your communication style do you feel were effective and
should be repeated in the future? Are there aspects of your communication style that you feel
would benefit from further development?

daily communication exchanges can teach you volumes about the kind of communicator
you are and what your current strengths and challenges might be.

Think about a recent exchange you have had with a family member in your early
childhood program that went well. What contributed to the success of the interaction?
Did you take time to carefully listen to what the family member had to say? Did you and
the individual seem to understand each other? Were points of disagreement resolved
quickly and with positive outcomes?

Pause again, this time thinking about a recent exchange that went poorly. Did you feel
you clearly communicated your message? Did you feel as if your points were not being
understood? Did you experience challenges in understanding where the other person
was coming from?

Successfully accomplishing relationship goals involves extending respect to all families; allowing families an equal voice in interactions; and acknowledging, appreciating, and incorporating family input. This chapter will focus on strategies to help you improve your communication and collaboration skills with the goal of developing respectful, reciprocal, responsive relationships with families. Communication and collaboration require learning specific skills and learning about yourself as a communicator. Not only do you need to explore how you communicate with others, but you also need to delve into why you might communicate in specific ways.

Setting Communication Goals

What is your greatest goal for communication? Is it to be understood? Is it to understand others? Is it combination of both—where there is an exchange based on mutual understanding? Ideally, communication supports reciprocity—we seek to understand others and want to be understood.

Truly understanding someone else can be a daunting task. Someone might hear my words, but do they grasp their meaning and the message that I am conveying? As a listener, I might be able to parrot back the words someone has spoken to me, but do I understand the underlying message? We can spend a great deal of time thinking that we understand someone perfectly, only to later realize that we have misunderstood his meaning. Many of our daily communication exchanges exist on the surface—routine, automatic communications where we hear words but do not truly listen or verbally make promises or connections that do not reflect our true intentions: "I'm fine," "That's great," "Sure," "Interesting," "Uh-huh," "Right," "Really?" These words can represent fillers that merely mark pauses in conversation, not true receipt of a message.

In the opening vignette, Myra begins her day excited to unveil her newly learned communication and collaboration skills. In the first communication exchange, she wants to talk with a mother about concerns regarding her daughter's development. Myra feels brushed off and unheard, but she has chosen to broach a sensitive topic at morning drop-off. On the surface, her choice of words may have served well as an introduction, but in terms of the context, her timing was off. When another parent approaches her at lunchtime, Myra communicates her distraction by her choice of filler words. The timing is not ideal for Myra, and she fails to adjust to the parent's need for communication. In her last exchange of the day, the moment the grandmother enters the room, Myra's defensiveness toward the grandmother is triggered. Her perception that the woman will never be happy with anything she does is so powerful that Myra feels it is not even worth responding to the grandmother's concerns.

Myra's goals for communication include connecting with others—to understand and be understood at a meaningful level. She understands that communication plays an important role in family access and participation in the early childhood environment. But she is also quickly learning that she needs to know more about successful communication; her success in connecting with others will require far more than knowledge of basic skills.

For families to truly engage in early childhood communities, connection is essential. Connection can only be attained when we each work to deeply understand what others are communicating and communicate with others from a place that represents our truest, most powerful selves. This power comes from speaking from our conscious, authentic self—who we are when we are at our best. When we communicate from this space, our words are shaped by integrity and empathy and infused with compassion. We bring our best selves to each interaction we engage in and respond to others with the respect that encourages them to communicate from their truest, most powerful selves. We set aside what we think we know and strive to discover and learn about ourselves, about others, and about the world we live in. In a world of miscommunications and misunderstandings where emotions can run high, communicating from our truest selves can be a challenge— there are so many distractions to saying what we truly mean and meaning what we say. One of the first steps in accomplishing meaningful, connected communication is to be mindful in your daily communications.

Defining Mindful Communication

Have you ever spoken with someone and felt that the person was just not present in the conversation? Perhaps he repeatedly checked his watch, looked over your shoulder at something behind you, said "Uh-huh" without regard for what you were saying, or stared into your eyes with a blank expression on his face. The person is there and appears to be responding to you but is not truly grounded in the exchange.

CHECKLIST FOR MINDFUL COMMUNICATION

I am fully present in the communication exchange, thinking about what is happening right now.

I am attending to what the other person is saying.

I recognize that the outcome of the exchange will be affected by how tuned in I am to the other person.

Successful communication requires that we mindfully participate in the exchange. The first step to mindful participation is to be fully present and attending.

When I am fully present in a communication exchange, I am in the moment and thinking about what the person I am communicating with is expressing. I might have a huge to-do list on my desk, seventeen things to buy at the grocery store, or a doctor's appointment for my child, but all of that is placed out of my mind as I am in the moment (fully present) and focused (attending). I have accepted that I am responsible for my contributions to this exchange and recognize that my focus will contribute to my understanding the message being communicated. Being fully present and attending to the person speaking communicates that what he has to say is important, that I respect him, and that I value his message. The speaker has the opportunity to be heard, and together we establish reciprocity. Being mindful is an important component of communication that engages families.

Being fully present and attending to communication exchanges is not without its challenges! Our world is fast paced and demanding, and we have constant pulls for our attention. Cell phones, email, instant messaging, and texting have taught us to communicate instantly and in short bursts. Taking time to ground yourself in focused communication might be a skill that at first requires a great deal of diligence to develop. Failure to develop these skills is to risk mindlessness.

What are some of the costs associated with mindlessness? According to Dan Huston, author of *Communicating Mindfully,* mindlessness contributes to the following:

missed opportunities to make connections and learn how others are thinking,

missed opportunities to explore new solutions to problems,

little opportunity to represent your best self, and

communicating a lack of respect to the communication partner.

When working with families, being mindful in the communication exchange clearly signals that you are open to what a family is communicating.

Developing Accurate Perceptions

Perceptions provide explanations for events or the actions of another person. Our perceptions are not always accurate; they are strongly shaped by unique schemas we have developed in the past. Schemas represent mental structures that consist of related bits of information. Once we put these bits of information together, we develop larger and more complex patterns of meaning (O'Hair and Wiemann, 2009). Schemas can become expected storylines and can tell us what we can generally expect in interactions—for example, when I pick up the phone and say, "Hello," I expect that someone will respond. When I let someone cut in front of me in the grocery store line, I expect that he will say, "Thank you." Because schemas represent general expectations, we do not often think of them or even recognize that we have them. For example, I do not consider the fact that I have a schema for what will happen when I pick up the phone and say, "Hello," until someone does not respond and I am confused. Schemas can represent a kind of unwritten code of expectations, and each individual has unique schemas of how the world should work.

The problem with schemas is that the storylines we create can be extremely limiting. I might make assumptions based on the words and actions of others: "That parent is looking over my shoulder when I am talking because he is not interested in what I am saying." "Marco's parents do not come to family conferences because they do not care about his development." Because schemas allow us to process information in an automatic fashion, they can make communication (or the lack of it) effortless (Huston, 2010). If I were to look beyond the storyline created by my schema, I might learn that the first parent looking over my shoulder was checking on his child; Marco's parents care deeply about his development but could not afford gas to attend the family conference. For me to move beyond my storyline in both cases, I would have to communicate further and disregard my initial perception.

Disregarding initial perceptions can be challenging! We often unconsciously respond emotionally to our perceptions of situations, and our emotional responses can be powerful. According to Paul Ekman, an expert on emotional responses and the author of *Emotions Revealed,* the emotional trigger can be complex but often can involve "very fast mental processes operating in a way that consciousness cannot enter." In other words, we are not even aware that we have made a judgment that has triggered our emotions. In turn, these emotions affect our actions. Mindful communication is challenging when the link between judgment, emotion, and action is unclear.

Consider Myra and the grandmother in the opening vignette. Myra hears the grandmother say, "I see he is messy again." But, what is Myra's grandmother truly communicating? What emotions are shaping her statement? It is Myra's responsibility to unearth what is being communicated. One of the initial steps Myra will need to take to build a respectful, reciprocal, responsive relationship is to carefully examine her own perceptions.

Myra feels she has already addressed the father's math concerns. She has an immediate judgment, and her resulting action is disengagement. She sees the grandmother and immediately judges that the woman will never be happy with her, and she emotionally responds. Her response includes not seeking additional information. In both cases, her ability to effectively communicate has been affected by a lack of mindfulness regarding her perceptions.

How can we become more mindful of this connection between judgment, emotion, and action?

    Recognize your initial impulses.

    Stop and think about your emotional reaction.

    Decide whether your initial reaction is accurate or inaccurate.

    Respond based on your assessment of the accuracy of your initial response.

Recognize your initial impulses and specifically stop and think about your emotional reactions within the context of communication exchanges (Huston, 2010). When you are interacting with a family member who is angry because his child had sand in her clothes the day before, do you feel your heart start to race? Does your face tighten or does a frown appear? Can you feel your head slightly shake or your blood pressure go up a notch? Stop and think. What are you reacting to—the fact that you disagree with what the parent is angry about? Or are you reacting to his anger? What specific perceptions are shaping your reaction? If you take the time to stop and think, you can mindfully look at whether or not those perceptions that triggered the emotions are in fact accurate or erroneous.

ETHICAL RESPONSIBILITIES TO FAMILIES

Even if I am having an emotional reaction that I feel is valid, I have a professional responsibility to develop and maintain relationships with families. At the grocery store, I might display my irritation with someone who cuts in front of me in line, but my ethical responsibilities to families, according to the NAEYC Code of Ethical Conduct, include the following:

Be familiar with the knowledge base related to working effectively with families, and stay informed through continuing education and training.

Develop relationships of mutual trust, and create partnerships with the families we serve.

Welcome all family members, and encourage them to participate in the program.

Listen to families, acknowledge and build upon their strengths and competencies, and learn from them as we support them in their task of nurturing children.

Respect the dignity and preferences of each family, and make an effort to learn about the family's structure, culture, language, customs, and beliefs.

Acknowledge families' child-rearing values and their right to make decisions for their children.

Share information about each child's education and development with families, and help them understand and appreciate the current knowledge base of the early childhood profession.

Help family members enhance their understanding of their children, and support the continuing development of their skills as parents.

Participate in building support networks for families by providing them with opportunities to interact with program staff, other families, community resources, and professional services.

Learning to Actively Listen

Active listening requires that you are engaged, focused, invested in, and attending to what the other person has to say (see Table 2.1). Your body communicates your interest as you lean in slightly, have open arms, and nod your head. You verbally communicate your interest by commenting, "Go on," "I see," or "Interesting" at important intervals in the conversation. You reflect the messages you hear from the speaker to make sure you are understanding the message correctly: "You seem concerned that he is messy." Active listening is respectful both to yourself as a communicator and to the person you are communicating with, as it makes it more likely that you will understand the message that the speaker is trying to convey.

TABLE 2.1: ACTIVE LISTENING

Strategies	Tips
Listen to what the speaker is saying.	What words is the speaker using to communicate his message? What feelings is he expressing? How is he responding to your message?
Be aware of your physical presence.	Are your arms open? Is your posture upright, communicating focus? Do your facial expressions show interest and focus?
Be aware of your eyes.	Are you looking at the speaker? Are you using your eyes to understand what the speaker might be thinking?
Use language appropriately.	Are your comments on topic and related to what the speaker has communicated? Do you ask questions to clarify your understanding of what the speaker has said? Do you add your own thoughts to connect your perceptions to his?

(Adapted from Garcia, Winner, and Crooke, 2011.)

In responding to the grandmother, Myra can use active listening to tap into what she is truly communicating. She can look directly at the grandmother, let her know that she is listening, and ask questions to check her understanding. But, Myra might hear the message and still not truly understand it. She can then use seeking and verifying skills to make sure she has accurately understood the message.

Using Seeking and Verifying Skills

Seeking requires that you gather information, and *verifying* means that you use that information to clearly understand messages. Use different types of questions to gather information about the speaker's point of view. When working with families, seeking and verifying skills can be important in identifying family strengths, concerns, priorities, and resources (see Table 2.2).

TABLE 2.2: SEEKING AND VERIFYING

Question Type	Tips
Closed questions	Used to obtain a short, specific response: "Are you ready to work on toilet learning with Janie?"
Open questions	Allow for freedom and choice in the response: "What is your biggest concern about Christian's development right now?"
Probing questions	Use *why* questions to help the speaker elaborate on a topic: "Why do you feel that Toby's learning the alphabet is your biggest priority right now?"
Leading questions	Used to imply a specific response: "You feel that the materials we have sent home in Spanish have been helpful?"
Reflective questions	Used to express empathy: "You seem frustrated that we are suggesting further assessment."
(Adapted from Winton et al., 2010.)	

Questioning can provide valuable information about a family's values and beliefs. When Myra uses seeking and verifying skills with the grandmother, for example, she learns that the grandmother is concerned that when her grandson looks messy, others may think that the grandmother is not taking good care of him. Myra also learns that the grandmother does not value the time the boy spends outside because she is concerned that he is not keeping up academically. The grandmother would prefer that outdoor time be spent on academics. Once Myra has gained this information, she then needs to make sure that she understands. Through verifying, she can restate the message as she understands it and make sure that understanding is correct: "You're concerned that his being messy at pickup makes it look like you aren't caring for him properly," or "Thank you for explaining that to me. So, you would like him working on his letters and numbers more?" In each case, Myra is restating what she believes the speaker's message is to check for accuracy, to get clarification, and to get validation before she proceeds with the interaction.

Once you have used questioning and clarification and validation, you can move to summarizing information. In summarizing, you provide an overview of the major highlights of what has been discussed. In Myra's interaction, she could say, "Okay, so we have agreed that we will make sure that Thomas washes more thoroughly after he is outside and that he has a change of clothes," or "It sounds like you are concerned about Thomas's academic development right now and would like for more emphasis to be placed on that."

Adopting a Clean-Slate Perspective

Not only do you need to learn how to understand the messages someone is communicating to you, but you also need to learn to understand your own reactions. Anytime you catch yourself thinking, "Well, he always…" or "That is just how she reacts…" or "Isn't that just typical," you are making an assumption. Assumptions are based on potentially faulty schema, and communication builds from there. Assumptions also contribute to selective perceptions, in which we expect certain things to happen or not happen in communication exchanges and, therefore, look for our interactions to fulfill those expectations. For example, if I always expect a coworker to interrupt me when I am speaking, I am likely to look for that behavior and disregard situations when that behavior

does not occur. When I assume, I stop looking for why certain behaviors might be happening and operate solely based on the explanation that I have previously arrived at in my head. To truly develop accurate perceptions of situations and to be open to new information and patterns of communication, we must mindfully seek explanations for behaviors.

The more aware you are of how you are interpreting the words and actions of others, the more choice you have in how you respond—you are moving from automatic to intentional. Described by Brown and Ryan (2003) as a *clean-slate perspective,* this process supports freeing yourself from your existing schemas. Each interaction becomes a fresh interaction that you approach without bias. In each communication exchange, you carefully tune in to each individual and your own perceptions, and then mindfully make choices about your reactions, accessing your truest, most powerful self. It is from this vantage point that you can truly join with and support families.

Using Joining and Supporting Skills

Joining and supporting requires building communication exchanges; informing communication partners of new, shared realities; and seeking consensus for how interactions will proceed. When we build communication, we are adding our own ideas to those of the other speaker. This lets the speaker know that there is some agreement and that you also have ideas to contribute: "I appreciate what you shared about Jillian's communication at home. I would love to see her interact with her brothers and sisters," or "I really like the idea of suggesting to his parents that they come observe him in the classroom, Josie. I think that snack time would be a great time for them to come." Building can be an important aspect of relationship development, as it validates the speaker and creates shared ideas.

In addition to building, informing is a skill that provides specific information and knowledge based on the needs of the speaker: "We have a great family support group. I can let you know when they meet," or "Sometimes children do communicate less when adjusting to a new environment." Informing, like each of the other skills mentioned, requires that you have carefully attended to the conversation, have been an active participant, and have built a relationship.

Finally, seeking consensus involves reaching agreement and stating clearly how the agreed-upon goals will be accomplished: "It sounds like everyone agrees that Alayna has many wonderful strengths. Let's look at our plan for the next few weeks as she continues to adjust to the classroom." Seeking consensus represents an important point in the communication feedback loop, involving checking realities and perceptions before moving forward.

Learning to Resolve Conflicts

Despite our best attempts at communication and collaboration, conflict will occasionally arise. Conflict emerges from differing perspectives; our different schemas and storylines can affect our ability to effectively communicate. Conflict itself is not problematic. Working through conflict can be a valuable and productive activity for everyone involved, serving to promote healthy problem solving and to strengthen relationships. Conflict, when resolved effectively, can be a catalyst for positive change. However, unresolved conflict can consume excessive amounts of time, energy, and emotion, serving to worsen an already bad situation or to harm relationships (O'Hair and Wiemann, 2011). Learning conflict resolution skills is essential work for early childhood educators.

Your ability to mindfully communicate, to be fully present and attentive to the communication exchange, will support your understanding of what the other person is trying to communicate to you. Think about Myra in her exchange with the father who was concerned about his child not being exposed to enough math: the fact that she was not fully present in the exchange only served to escalate the conflict between them.

Understanding your schemas and your emotional responses to these schemas plays a key role in conflict resolution. If you understand what you are thinking and your emotional response, you are more likely to be able to rationally act and respond. You can carefully assess if you are responding to the situation in front of you or to an existing storyline. The more carefully you become aware of the link between judgment, emotion, and action, the more likely you are to be a full partner in the exchange.

Resolving conflict requires reciprocity. You might be aware of your contributions to the communication exchange, but you also need to actively listen to fully understand where the other person is coming from. You need to use your seeking and verifying skills to make sure that you have gathered information about the speaker's perspective and that you clearly understand the message.

Once you fully understand the other person's perspective, conflict resolution requires the introduction of a new perspective. Described by Barrera, Corso, and Macpherson (2003) as the third space, adopting this perspective allows me to view the conflict or contradiction in a different light. The third space allows for a new perspective based on shared realities. For example, a parent might think a toddler should be fed by the teacher during meal times, while the teacher might believe that it is important for the child to learn to serve herself. Creating a third space in this situation could include exploring how to support the child's developing independence skills in the classroom and at home. Instead of choosing one or another person's point of view, the third space is an opportunity for dialogue and a new way of thinking based on a merging of shared views, not based on my or your perspective but on a new, shared perspective that reflects our respectful, responsive communication. "A third-space perspective does not 'solve the problem.' Rather it changes the arena within which that problem is addressed by increasing the probability of respectful, responsive, and reciprocal interactions. In so doing, an optimal response to the situation becomes more likely" (Barrera, Corso, and Macpherson, 2003). Once you identify the other person's perspective, together you can create a new, shared reality through joining and supporting.

When resolving conflicts, adopt a spectrum of potential solutions rather than an either-or outcome. A spectrum implies that you are open to a realm of possibilities—that your schemas and ways of interpretation are willing to expand and that your actions will expand as well. Everyone's voice and values are heard and respected. In this way, conflict provides an opportunity for growth.

Chapter Reflection Questions

What is your greatest goal for communication?

What do you feel are your strengths when communicating with others?

What communication areas do you feel most need strengthening?

What action steps can you identify from information shared in this chapter that will support your becoming a more effective communicator?

How can you apply conflict-resolution skills shared in this chapter to an existing conflict?

Questions to Explore with Families

What is your greatest goal for communication?

What strategies do others use when communicating that lead you to believe your message is important to them?

What is your general preference for addressing conflicts when they arise?

What strategies have you found most beneficial in resolving conflict?

Understanding Social Identities and Cultural Frameworks

CHAPTER 3

Defining Social Identity

Our unique social identities provide a cultural framework that serves as an invisible "windshield" affecting how we see the world. Learning about our own unique identities and the richness and complexities of diverse family identities are keys to effective communication and collaboration. When we understand our own perspective and the perspectives of others, we can create respectful, reciprocal, responsive environments that truly engage each family.

The term *social identity* refers to how we define ourselves as members of a group (Deaux, 2001). Our social identity shapes our response to the question, "Who am I?" This response can be guided by many factors:

    race,

    gender,

    age,

    varied abilities,

language,

ethnicity,

national origin,

social class, including our level of education and occupation,

religiosity and/or spiritual beliefs,

the region of the country that we live in,

political affiliations; and

sexuality, including our sexual orientation.

What each person uses to define her identity is unique to that individual. For example, two colleagues might belong to similar groups, but each may place different values on her self-identification with these groups. Both people might be female, Catholic, and Latina, but one may strongly identify with her Latina heritage and the other more strongly with her Catholic identity.

While some aspects of a person's social identity are chosen by that person, others are ascribed or given by circumstances or by other people. Examples of ascribed social identities can include gender, race, or being the parent of a child with a disability. When others see a person as belonging to a specific group, their beliefs about that group can affect how they view and interact with the individual.

Whether a social identity is chosen or ascribed, each aspect of our social identity can serve both to connect us to other people and distinguish us from other groups. The language an individual speaks, for example, can provide membership and inclusion through communication to one group as well as serve as a source of potential exclusion from another group. For example, Gregory, an early childhood teacher, speaks Spanish, which connects him to other Spanish speakers. He did not learn to speak English until he was in the sixth grade. While his English skills were developing, he could communicate with other Spanish speakers but was excluded from communication with individuals who only spoke English.

Social identities provide labels, but with these labels come cognitive beliefs (what we think about these labels), emotional associations (how we feel about these labels), and behavioral consequences (how we act relative to these labels).

STEREOTYPES

One of the main dangers with ascribed social identities is stereotyping. When we stereotype, we lump individuals into one-dimensional categories based on external characteristics, ignoring unique experiences and complexities of individual lives (Ngo, 2008). In the United States, for example, individuals share the same nationality but may be from many different ethnic backgrounds. People who share a particular ethnic identity may share some cultural traits and group history but might vary in religious traits, foods and customs, or language. To make assumptions based on ethnicity is to ignore the rich and unique meaning people bring to their individual lives.

An individual might think, feel, and act a particular way based on his identification with a group. I am the parent of a child with a disability, for example, and strongly identify with this role as a passionate advocate for issues affecting children with disabilities. This social identity has strengthened my sense of who I am and has further defined my personal and professional roles. I am incredibly proud of my daughter, support her independence, and actively seek resources that will help her continue to develop and thrive. This social identity has provided me with amazing life lessons about what it is to be human and has enriched my life immeasurably.

Another person who shares the social identity of being a parent of a child with a disability, however, might not identify with that role in the same way that I do—her internal factors, such as cognitive beliefs, emotional associations, and behavioral actions, may differ. For example, if a person believes that her child's disabilities are a source of punishment for the family, then her resulting emotional associations may include shame. She may not choose to actively participate in early intervention and related special education services, as she thinks that child's disability represents something that the family brought upon themselves. A teacher who understands the links among cognitive beliefs, emotional associations, and behavioral actions can use that information and understanding as she seeks to connect and work with that family.

My daughter, who has many amazing strengths and—similar to any child—some challenges, includes in her social identity the reality that she has muscular dystrophy. Some of the disadvantages of this group membership are imposed on her by others and, therefore, are shaped by external factors. Society views her as having a disability. According to Nieto and Boyer (2010), others might judge, stereotype, or even demand conformity from some groups to the majority. Demands for conformity can take the form of institutional biases, racism, or discrimination.

Gregory strongly identifies with his role as an early childhood educator, yet feels judged by many families for being a male within the profession. He feels the strongest sense of identification when communicating with other men who have chosen this occupation. Many gay and lesbian parents might feel judged within their role as parents but may feel strong positive feelings when interacting with other gay and lesbian parents (Deaux, 2001). Andrew Solomon, in his book *Far from the Tree: Parents, Children, and the Search for Identity,* writes that, for many children with exceptionalities, positive identification and group membership happens when the children connect with others who share strengths and challenges that are similar to their own. Bias and discrimination from larger society can be marked.

Understanding How Perception Influences Actions

Teachers' perceptions and actions can affect the social identities of families. Lela and Gregory's infant/toddler classroom is filled with children from diverse backgrounds. The teachers work hard to learn about each child: the languages spoken in the home, where the child lives, who the child lives with, and other basic demographic information. Their classroom has a variety of books that they consider diverse and dolls in the housekeeping area that look like the children in their care, the families, and the members of their community. The pictures on the walls show people living in various places, of various backgrounds, and with varied abilities. Lela and Gregory also implement an anti-bias curriculum and work to incorporate the children's home languages into their classroom environment.

The teachers feel that their work with families needs further development—their goal is to communicate to each child and family that they truly belong and to develop respectful, reciprocal, responsive relationships. However, they do not always see eye to eye on how to best do this. Lela and Gregory often debate with each other about parenting practices and are unclear about how their own ideas of effective practices align with the families of the children. The teachers debate about toilet learning, guidance, self-serve snack—it seems that they have many issues of disagreement. Despite their disagreements, the teachers have a shared vision of creating an environment where each family feels truly engaged and where they and the families can mutually affect each other's lives and the classroom community.

Lela and Gregory work with two families who are currently living in poverty. Lela believes that the children in these families are being raised within a culture of poverty and that the parents will instill values and behaviors that will cause the children to live in poverty when they reach adulthood. Gregory, on the other hand, feels that the families' living situations are created by a pervasive lack of access to resources. Each of the teachers has unique perceptions based on his or her social identities, and each believes that his or her perspective is correct. It is not hard to imagine how these different perceptions might affect interactions with the families. In Lela's case, her focus is on how the family is not instilling the appropriate values, and her energies are channeled toward that. In Gregory's

ISSUES OF OPPORTUNITY: POVERTY

Every day, five-year-old Mandy and her family struggle to get ahead. She lives in a community where her school lacks highly qualified teachers and where staff turnover is high. Their family does not regularly access health services, and Mandy is often sick from preventable illnesses. Her family struggles to put food on the table. When Mandy was three, she, her two brothers, and her parents briefly experienced homelessness. She is not allowed to go outside and play because her neighborhood is unsafe. Although both her parents work, the wages they earn are barely enough for them to scrape by.

Children living in poverty comprise 21 percent of all children living in the United States (National Center for Children in Poverty, 2012). Culturally, these families are often viewed through a deficit perspective, that their poverty is due to personal and moral deficiencies and that pervasive poverty continues because of cultural choices.

To move beyond the deficit perspective and provide meaningful support to families, consider the following:
  Identify the obstacles the families face and connect families with appropriate supports and resources, help families negotiate paperwork, and work to help them integrate supports successfully into their life.
  Examine classroom policies and practices: Does Show and Tell, where children bring objects from home, highlight differential access to material wealth? Do family conferences and family nights take into account that some families might work multiple jobs? Are these events scheduled at convenient, flexible times?
  Emphasize a strengths-based perspective, recognize the incredibly challenging conditions that persons who live in poverty must deal with, and seek ways to support and strengthen the resiliency it takes to push, strive, and learn in the face of these obstacles (Gorski, 2007).

It is important to keep in mind that families may be reluctant to engage with the school or may distrust the intentions of teachers. This does not reflect a lack of value for education (Gorski, 2007). Rather, these reactions might be based on a history of feeling marginalized within the system.

case, his energies are devoted to making sure the family is connected with needed resources. Research, by the way, supports Gregory's point of view: there is no evidence that a culture of poverty exists—differences in values and behaviors among persons who are poor are just as great as among those who are wealthy (Gorski, 2007).

As educators, we are interacting with families based on our social identities as early childhood teachers. Families interact with us in their roles as parents and caregivers of their children. While many of our unique social identities affect our roles as professionals— it is impossible for me to separate myself as a professional from myself as a woman— there are other aspects of our social identities that may not be appropriate within the professional arena. For example, a teacher's political affiliation would not be appropriate or relevant to her professional role or the relationships she builds within it.

Our social identities provide us with a *cultural framework*—the way we process and see the world.

Understanding Cultural Frameworks

Our social identities provide us with a complex, elusive, and fascinating cultural framework. We each belong to various cultures, and our membership provides us with our own unique lens to the world. We are often not even aware that we have a unique cultural lens, nor are we aware of how this lens affects our communication with others. Our cultural view of the world changes depending on the context that we are in and our interactions with others. Learning about the social identities that comprise our own culture and the culture of others is an important part of creating environments that support the access and full participation of the families we work with.

We often use the term *culture* to represent the outward and internal representations of our social identities. Culture in the larger sense is the learned and shared knowledge that individual members of specific groups use to shape their behaviors and process their unique experiences of the world (Gilbert, Goode, and Dunne, 2007). Religious groups can have a culture. Your ethnic background might be associated with a specific culture. The fact that you are male or female can influence your cultural outlook. A person who is deaf might be an active participant in deaf culture. Culture includes such things as how groups of people communicate, the rituals that punctuate their daily lives, the roles they enact, their beliefs, how courtesies are extended, their individual customs, their ways of interacting, and their expectations for behaviors. Culture serves as the context that provides us with a schema of who we are and how we represent ourselves to others, as well as how we interpret who other people are. So much of the cultural knowledge that we each have gained is through our unique interactions with other members of our group (Maschinot, 2008). It can be difficult to identify the cultural components of our worldview and recognize how this affects interactions with others.

Developing Cultural Literacy

We each develop cultural literacy within our own cultures as we master verbal and nonverbal cues, what has meaning within the social environment (contextual knowledge), cultural symbols, and how we should interact with others (Borden, 1991). Learning about one's own culture is an active and dynamic process, and classes begin on the day you are born. We are unlikely to even realize that we have knowledge of culture, as it is something that we take for granted. Knowledge of our own culture is often treated as "just how things are"—something that we accept as a reality that exists for everyone. It is often not until we interact with individuals whose culture differs from our own that we begin to recognize that we have our own unique cultural lens.

Consider Lela, who is a primary caregiver for a small group of children. Lela believes that children should be held every day before being placed down for a nap, gently rocked until they are almost completely asleep, then placed in their cribs where they can drift the rest of the way to sleep independently. The parents of Chara, a child in Lela's class, want Chara placed in the crib at the same time every day and allowed to cry until she falls asleep. Think about the differing perspectives: Do you feel that one strategy is better than the other? Is the practice of how a child should be put to sleep something you can remember being specifically taught, or is this knowledge that you just somehow know to be true? Do you think that there are any values that underlie preferences for how a child should be put to sleep? If so, what do you think these values might be?

How to put a baby to sleep is one of many examples of how culture might affect child-rearing preferences and practices. Feeding practices, how

LOOKING THROUGH YOUR CULTURAL LENS: THINKING ABOUT YOUR UNDERLYING VALUES

Think about a common daily routine in early childhood classrooms, such as nap time procedures, diapering, self-serve snack, transitions, or getting ready to go outside.

Reflect on whether or not you have expectations for how the routine should occur. Are there certain behaviors you expect of the children? Are there certain goals that you work to develop? What are these?

Now think about where these expectations and goals came from. What do you think led you to feel that these were most appropriate?

Consider the families in your classroom environment. Does each family have shared expectations and goals for their children?

If the answer is no to the above question, or if you are not sure, how might varied expectations and goals affect your communication with these family members?

children are played with, guidance interactions, and toilet learning are other examples. Before we explore in more depth how your culture and the culture of families you work with might affect engagement, let's take a closer look at the concept of cultural diversity.

Understanding Cultural Diversity

We develop our cultural framework based on our social identities. In the United States, we live in a diverse society where there is a shared culture (called a *macroculture*) and many subcultures (referred to as *microcultures*). Similar to diversity in our social identities, any individual might participate in the framework of the macroculture as well as microcultural groups. Therefore, many identify with more than one culture, or even two or more distinct cultures (Seeye and Wasilewski, 1996).

Just as your training in early childhood education has provided you with a social identity, it has also provided you with a culture. Through your studies, you have learned a European-American perspective of healthy or typical development (Golden, 2011) and evidence-based strategies for ensuring that children and families attain positive developmental outcomes.

LEARNING ABOUT A FAMILY'S UNDERLYING VALUES

Brainstorm questions you can use to learn more about a family's underlying values for caregiving:

❖ Open questions: "What do you feel is the most effective way to put your child down for a nap?"

❖ Probing questions: "Why do you feel allowing the child to be rocked might be a problem?"

❖ Reflective questions: "You are concerned about nap-time procedures, correct? Let's spend some time talking about this."

Explore how you can validate the information the family has provided to you:

❖ "I am hearing that you are afraid Chara will become dependent."

❖ "It sounds like you are concerned that Chara will expect that at night, too, and you don't have time to rock her with three other children."

Move to summarizing the information based on your discussion:

❖ "So, we have discussed our waiting a bit longer to put Chara down for a nap and trying to have her just drift off to sleep without being rocked or crying."

Your cultural perspective may not be shared by all families in your program. Lela, for example, believes she knows the most effective way to place children down for a nap and that the strategy she uses nurtures and supports children's developing autonomy. Chara's parents, however, feel that the most effective way to support Chara's development is to allow their child to cry it out. They believe this approach will allow their child to become more self-reliant and adept at soothing herself. Ultimately, they feel this strategy will result in increased independence and will support positive developmental outcomes for Chara.

Which perspective is accurate? In which scenario are there more likely to be positive developmental outcomes? You might feel that the answer is clear, but keep in mind that someone else reading the scenario might feel strongly about the opposing viewpoint. Both the families you work with and other professionals might not have the same vision for supporting children's development as you, nor may they share the same strategies for supporting children in attaining that vision (Golden, 2011). Their cultural perspectives may differ.

In addition to understanding the components of culture, it is important to understand how culture manifests itself. We are often unaware of the constant and consuming affect culture has in shaping our daily lives. As the windshield we see the world through, culture not only affects our perceptions of the world, but how we process and respond to it.

Recognizing Our Personal Cultural Lens

Schemas, the mental structures that provide us with storylines and tell us what we can expect in interactions, influence our cultural lens. We are often unaware of the schemas we hold. Learning about this lens and its effect on our interactions with others can be challenging, as there are several realities of cultural programming (Gardenswartz and Rowe, 1998) that require attention:

Culture is not overt. We do not recognize cultural rules until a rule is broken. Different cultures, for example, have different codes for *proxemics,* the distance you should stand from someone when communicating. You might not have any idea what the exact distance is, but you know that you are uncomfortable when communicating with someone who is a close talker.

In addition to not knowing what cultural rules are, we are often not aware when looking at someone what that person's culture is. We might even erroneously make assumptions about someone's culture based on appearance. Each of these factors can make cultural missteps likely.

We are all basically ethnocentric. We feel that our own culture is better than others. This relates to the idea that we often accept culture as truth: "This is how things should be," or "They should not act like that." As culture is deeply rooted and something that we learn about through immersion from birth, we tend to accept our realities as truths, not recognizing that others experience totally different realities.

We tend to observe, interpret, then act. We can misinterpret the actions of others by not understanding their cultural norms. Misinterpretation is likely if our observations are based on existing schemas and peppered with judgment. We may not know when we are offending others and, therefore, might not have the opportunity to learn from and correct cultural miscues.

LOOKING THROUGH YOUR CULTURAL LENS:

LEARNING ABOUT YOUR OWN CULTURAL PROGRAMMING

Carefully observe the effect of your interactions on others, watching for their reactions. Also take careful note of your reactions to how others interact with you. What can you learn about your own reactions? Think about the things that you accept as deep-seated truths—an indication of these beliefs is when you have the word *should* attached to something. Where do you think these beliefs come from? What might these shoulds teach you about your own belief system? What might be the outcome if your belief system is not the same as someone else's?

How carefully do you think about why people are acting in a particular way? Do you look outside your own assumptions for alternative explanations or assume that you understand the root causes of people's behavior?

Overcoming these realities of cultural programming begins with awareness and knowledge (Gardenswartz and Rowe, 1998). Being aware of differences and potential barriers allows greater choice in how we interact with others and greater potential for successful interactions. Consider again the concept of the clean-slate perspective, from Chapter 2. Through adopting this perspective, you are able to greet each interaction as a fresh interaction, free from cultural programming and existing storylines. How can these realities of cultural programming be used to increase our own self-awareness and knowledge, and thereby decrease our biases?

In her book *The Changing Face of the United States: The Influence of Culture on Child Development,* Beth Maschinot advocates developing awareness of cultural scripts. Where schemas provide us with an initial storyline and related perceptions, cultural scripts place these storylines in context and serve as tools that guide us in solving human problems. Child rearing—a challenging task—is one area where these scripts are powerful. Scripts provide us with a compass for the way things ought to be done and give us a pervasive and strong worldview. Children "should" behave in a particular way; families "should" stress certain behaviors with their children; children "should" have certain routines. Gregory, the early childhood teacher, examined his cultural scripts and found that they were riddled with shoulds: Families should always be home with their children if they have a day off. Families should always encourage children to do things for themselves. Families should always have children in bed by what he considered a reasonable hour. When thinking about the families in his classroom, Gregory realized that many of his cultural scripts did not align with theirs, and he spent a great deal of time and energy tending to these shoulds in his head and in conversations with Lela, his teaching partner. Our cultural scripts might be particularly strong if we are middle-class European Americans, where the scripts that we hold regarding child rearing are unlikely to be challenged by our education in the field of early childhood education or the larger culture (Maschinot, 2008).

We each need to become more aware of how cultural scripts affect our relationships with families. To do this, look carefully at situations where your internal responses are "I know" or "I am sure." Consider replacing those certainties with "What if": What if there were a different way to view this child's development? What if there were other strategies that would be most supportive of this child in this family's context? The idea is to not only explore what you currently believe, but also to really examine what meaning is shaping that belief system (Barrera and Corso, 2002). Only when we truly understand the lens that we bring to the situation can we hope to effectively partner with families.

OPEN-ENDED QUESTIONS TO LEARN MORE ABOUT FAMILIES' CULTURAL SCRIPTS

What are your hopes and dreams for your child?

When your child engages in (X) behavior, what does it mean to you?

What are your overall goals for your child's behavior and development?

What are your goals for your child as an adult?

Understanding the Cultural Lenses of Families

In addition to learning about your own cultural lens, it is essential to learn about the cultural lenses of families. This includes learning about their world from their perspective and becoming curious about the cognitive and emotional frameworks that they shape and process their world through (Barrera and Corso, 2002). Take the time to truly learn about the family's goals for their child's development and how those goals translate into the family's vision of the child as an adult (Rosenthal and Roer-Strier, 2001). What are the family's plans, hopes, and dreams for their child at present as well as in the future? Use focused attention, patience, and curiosity to learn more about the families you work with and the cultural scripts that guide their behavior.

Lela and Gregory are becoming increasingly aware that they need to learn more about their own cultural scripts as well as the cultural scripts of the families in their care. Both are learning that their own social identities, including their identification with the field of early childhood education, shape their cultural scripts of what should happen as they support children's learning and development within the early childhood classroom. But their cultural scripts and those of the families they work with are not always the same. They feel that their understandings of culture and how it influences interactions only scratch the surface.

Identifying the Complexities of Culture

Kalyanpur and Harry (2012) identify three levels of cultural awareness that require our attention within early childhood environments. Levels that are least likely to receive our support include covert and subtle levels of cultural awareness. Covert levels include status (how the role of the teacher is viewed, or how the role of the parent is seen within the early childhood community) or communication styles (preference for greetings, eye contact, body posture). Subtle levels include recognizing the embedded values and beliefs that underlie people's actions, such as parenting values and how these shape goals for children's behavior.

The overt level of cultural awareness includes where and how people live, style of dress, food preferences, and speech patterns. These explicit aspects of culture are ones we are much more likely to take note of and pay attention to in early childhood environments.

Lela and Gregory incorporate overt aspects of culture into their early childhood environments by including clothes from families' cultures in the housekeeping area and pictures of the various places that children call home on the walls of the classroom. Incorporating only overt aspects of culture has challenges, however. Representations of how children and families live their daily lives can be stereotyped based on group membership. Focusing on overt aspects may mean missing opportunities for deeper connection provided through connecting at covert and subtle levels.

In terms of stereotyping based on group membership, a program or classroom might assume that because a child or family belongs to a certain group, certain activities and practices are reflective of their lives. For example, Lela and Gregory decide to celebrate Cinco de Mayo because there is a family of Mexican descent in their program. However, they learn that this particular holiday and the way it is celebrated does not have any meaning for that particular family.

When Lela and Gregory tune in to the family at the subtle level of cultural awareness, they learn that the family is concerned that their child has been repeatedly saying no to his parents at home since he has entered the program. The family sees the program's emphasis on independence as something that is undermining their parenting at home. Before Lela and Gregory had meaningful discussions with the family about family goals and program and classroom practices, the teachers were unaware that the family felt their cultural values were being undermined. As far as the teaching staff was concerned, they were going to address issues of culture related to this family through their Cinco de Mayo celebration! Had they not connected at the subtle level, opportunities for meaningful communication would have been lost.

USING QUESTIONING AND ACTIVE LISTENING SKILLS TO LEARN ABOUT FAMILY VALUES AND GOALS

Before planning classroom and program events, use open questions to learn more about meaningful cultural practices in families' lives and if and how they would like these practices included. Use probing and open-ended questions to learn about goals for children's development. Actively listen to what the family is communicating, showing verbal and nonverbal interest and reflecting the messages you hear from the speaker.

Awareness of cultural differences is one aspect of developing respectful, reciprocal, responsive relationships that serve to meaningfully engage families within early childhood environments. Learning about the underlying beliefs and values that create the difference is another, often overlooked aspect (Kalyanpur and Harry, 2012). For the family and program described in the above example, Lela and Gregory need to explore the factors that shape their own value for independence and where that value originates: Why do they feel independence plays an important role in supporting the child's development and learning? The teachers, in turn, also need to learn more about the family's values and goals for their child.

Our cultural framework, like our social identities, is not a static factor, but is something that is dynamic and ever changing based on interactions with others in the world around us (Bennett et al., 2001). Individuals are affected by their immediate cultural groups and by the macroculture as well. There is a fluidity to culture, which involves different expectations and different ways of acting and interacting across the various contexts we find ourselves in. We each as individuals, for example, might act one way in our homes, another way at our place of work, and another way with our friends. When engaging families, it is important to keep in mind that the culture of the early childhood community may differ greatly from the home environment, with different ways of interacting, different rules, and varied expectations for behaviors. Teachers can learn a great deal about families by asking them about the following:

How do family members interact within the home?

What are the rules that children are expected to follow within the home?

What are general expectations for their child's behavior?

Social identities contribute to the development of a cultural framework. Teachers can use knowledge about families' cultural frameworks to form successful partnerships as a foundational step in engaging families within the classroom community.

Chapter Reflection Questions

What are important aspects of your own social identities?

What cognitive beliefs (what you think), emotional associations (how you feel), and behavioral consequences (how you act) are associated with your social identities?

How do your social identities influence your professional role?

What are your underlying values for each of the following routines: nap times, diapering, and guidance? Do the families in your program share these values?

What strategies can you use to learn about a family's underlying values and goals?

When do you hear yourself using "should" with regard to your professional role?

What does your use of "shoulds" teach you about your own cultural programming?

What strategies can you use to connect with families at the covert and subtle levels of cultural awareness?

Questions to Explore with Families

What do you feel is the most effective way to put a child down for a nap, diaper a child, or guide a child's behavior? Why do you feel these strategies are most appropriate? What are your hopes and dreams for your child?

When your child engages in (X) behavior, what does it mean to you?

What are your overall goals for your child's behavior and development?

What are your goals for your child as an adult?

Becoming a Culturally Competent Communicator

CHAPTER 4

The McMahan family has three children. Aidan, their youngest, is a four-year-old in Mary Irene and Josie's preschool classroom. Aidan seemed to adjust to the preschool class well, easily separating from his parents and eagerly participating in classroom activities. From the start, his teachers noticed that Aidan preferred to communicate nonverbally, using gestures to indicate most of his needs. They are not sure if his communication style is a cause for concern.

Based on their center's policy, the teachers used the Ages and Stages Questionnaire (ASQ) after Aidan was in the program for two weeks to assess his overall development. To gather information about his development within the home environment, Mary Irene and Josie also gave a copy of the ASQ to his parents to complete. After the teachers had compiled their scores and the parent portion, they found that Aidan scored low in the communication domain. The teachers met with Aidan's parents to talk about the screening results. One of their goals was to emphasize the importance of taking the screening results to Aidan's pediatrician to have a more formal assessment completed.

When the teachers met with the parents, however, they were surprised by their reaction. After going through the items and listening to the explanation of the results, the parents indicated that they thought Aidan's communication was "just fine… nothing a bit of time won't fix." When the teachers stressed the importance of early identification and the potential benefits Aidan might gain from early intervention, the parents responded that they were not interested, saying, "We have way too much on our plates right now to pursue this."

This vignette is an example of a challenge that can occur when working with families. At the core of the situation is a dilemma: the teachers and the parents differ on what next steps might be helpful to Aidan. Mary Irene and Josie will need to rely on their communication and collaboration skills to resolve this dilemma with the family.

The term *culture* refers to such things as how people communicate, their rituals, the roles they enact, the languages used, their beliefs, how courtesies are extended, their customs, ways of interacting, and expected behaviors. We each have unique social identities that make up our cultural frameworks. Our social identities include such factors as our race, ethnicity, religion, politics, gender, sexual orientation, age, education, role, occupation, varied abilities, the region of the country we live in, and so on. When we use the term *cultural competency,* we are referring to harmonious behaviors, attitudes, policies, structures, and practices that help us to work effectively in cross-cultural situations such as the following:

> classroom and program policies and practices,
> how classrooms and teachers support children and families, and
> how individuals act and interact with each other.
> (Adapted from Cross et al., 1989.)

We establish mutual respect and reciprocity when we work effectively in cross-cultural situations to create harmony and when programs and individuals are responsive to family needs. This synergy creates a climate for family engagement. A lack of harmony creates discord—families and staff do not feel that they are respected by one another, there is no opportunity for reciprocity, and responsiveness is not an option. Attaining cultural competency requires communication.

Engaging in culturally competent communication means that you understand many factors:

What is the effect of your cultural framework on your communication with others?

How do the cultural frameworks of those you are communicating with influence their communication?

What is the overall context of communication, and how does this influence your communication?

Many different messages can be communicated and received within the complicated and multifaceted context of communication. The message you think you are communicating is not always the message being received, just as the message you are receiving is not always the message intended. If your message is not accurately conveyed, and you do not understand the message communicated, miscommunication has occurred. Failing to understand how culture shapes communication can contribute to miscommunication.

Understanding How Culture Influences Communication

The relationship between culture and communication is complex. We are each surrounded by culture and live deep within it; culture permeates every aspect of our lives. It is the intangible aspects of culture, the covert and subtle details, which are much more difficult for us to navigate in communication, as these are often transparent and invisible. We are likely, for example, to understand and respond to an individual's primary language and dialect, where we might recognize the need for translation or interpretation services. We also are likely to pick up on volume and tone, which relay words as well as emotion. We may assume, for example, that a parent who speaks in a loud voice when we call to tell her that her child bumped his head is angry. Similarly, we may assume that a parent who reacts with an excited cadence and smiles when we share that his child wrote her name is happy. We are less likely to pick up on more covert, nonverbal forms of communication, which include such things as the following:

choice and degree of disclosure—how much an individual shares about her personal life;

permission of touch—how comfortable an individual is touching another and being touched;

boundaries of personal space—how close one stands when interacting with others;

use of gestures;

facial expressions;

permissibility of eye contact—when it is acceptable to look someone else in the eye or to look away; and

preferred greetings (Long, 2011).

Even subtler are cultural communication patterns surrounding temporal relationships, including how an individual views time. This includes the use of time in relationship to others (timeliness and responding to deadlines), as well as how individuals ground and refer to themselves in the past, present, and future. Some individuals, for example, might be focused on the past in terms of how they define themselves and their relationships with others: "Our family has overcome many challenges." Others may be very engaged in the present: "Right now, we are working on the following goals…" Other individuals might be oriented toward the future: "Our hopes for the future include…" (Long, 2011). Understanding temporal relationships helps us to understand how families think and feel about a particular situation regarding their child, as well as how they feel about the future. For example, you and a family in your classroom might differ in your goals for the child. You might have long-term goals in mind, such as supporting independence and autonomy. The family, on the other hand, might be focused on short-term goals—they see the child's success within your classroom as based on how happy the child is. The family is not currently focused on future independence. Your varied perspectives regarding temporal goals can result in a miscommunication. Understanding this can give you insight into why some of your communication strategies may be ineffective. You are more likely to gain a meaningful response from the family if you frame communication within temporal goals that are meaningful to them.

It is important to understand covert and subtle communication preferences. Reflect on each of the following and what they indicate about your communication preferences:

How much do you reveal about yourself personally in your interactions with others?

How comfortable are you when others reveal personal information about themselves?

How do you use touch in your interactions with others? How open and comfortable are you touching others and being touched in professional relationships?

What amount of personal space are you comfortable maintaining when you interact with others? How do you feel when someone stands too close or far away from you? How do you use your hands to communicate when you interact with others? What kinds of facial expressions do you use in your interactions? How does this enhance or impede your communication with others? If you are unsure, talk with a trusted friend or colleague who will give you an honest evaluation.

Do you look people directly in the eye when communicating with them? How do you feel when others look you in the eye or look away from you when communicating? How do you greet others? Do you use a handshake or a hug? How do you prefer to be greeted? How do you feel when people greet you in ways that deviate from your preferences? How timely are you? Do you arrive at appointments promptly and consistently make deadlines? What are your expectations for others in terms of timeliness? When you communicate with others, do you typically use language that refers to the past, present, or future? How does this affect the goals that you have for yourself and those who are close to you?

Culture not only influences how we communicate with one another but also the content of our communication. Content is influenced through the cultural scripts we carry. Cultural scripts represent schemas in context. While schemas provide us with an initial storyline and related perceptions, cultural scripts place these storylines in context and serve as tools that guide us in solving human problems. Our cultural scripts provide us with information about feeding, sleeping, eating, communication, discipline, exploring and learning, and fostering independence or interdependence (Hepburn, 2004). These scripts serve as a kind of map that guides our expectations. Our scripts and those of families might differ greatly—a family might value cosleeping as a way to foster interdependence in their child, while a caregiver may strongly value a child sleeping in his own bed as a way to foster independence. The scripts that we hold surrounding these practices can be quite powerful and emotionally charged. When thinking about the context of communication, attention to cultural scripts is critical.

Your cultural scripts regarding the care and education of young children are shaped by your role and the education you received in preparing for this role—early childhood education is a culture. Think about Mary Irene and Josie in the vignette. They have cultural knowledge of screening, assessment, and early intervention. This is information they have learned and hold to be true based on their education within the early childhood field. Mary Irene and Josie have deep knowledge of the screening and assessment process— they understand each of the steps involved as well as the different possible outcomes. They also understand the importance and benefits of early intervention. Aidan's family does not share this knowledge; the cultural knowledge that Mary Irene and Josie have adds a dimension to their communication with the family. The teachers' and the family's perspectives on what Aidan needs differ. If these teachers fail to recognize that they are responding from a cultural perspective that does not represent shared knowledge and even a shared reality, the potential for miscommunication is great.

Learning about Your Cultural Scripts

Explore some of your cultural scripts regarding the field of early childhood education, perspectives that you might take for granted. As you reflect on each of the following, think about your knowledge source for your response: What body of knowledge are you drawing on to shape your answer to the prompt?

> What is the most effective way to structure feeding for a small group of children—self-serve, family style, teacher served, another method?
> What is the best way to put a child down for a nap?
> What are effective communication strategies with families?
> What are guidance practices that support a sense of classroom community?
> What is the role of play in the classroom environment?
> How should the classroom be structured to support child exploration and interaction?
> How much should children be encouraged to complete tasks on their own?

Understanding the effect of your cultural scripts requires thinking about your own cultural scripts, the cultural scripts of others, and the *interaction* between your cultural scripts and those of the individuals around you (see Table 4.1).

TABLE 4.1: HOW CULTURAL SCRIPTS INFLUENCE COMMUNICATION

Learning about Yourself	Learning about Others	Learning about Context of Interactions
How are your own attitudes about such subjects as feeding, sleeping, eating, communication, discipline, play, exploring and learning, and fostering independence or interdependence similar to or different from those that you learned in your own family? In what ways do you communicate your cultural scripts in your interactions with families? In what ways are your cultural scripts reflected within the early childhood environment?	What do you know about each family's cultural scripts related to feeding, sleeping, eating, communication, discipline, play, exploring and learning, and fostering independence or interdependence? In what ways are each family's cultural scripts reflected in their parenting beliefs and practices?	How do your cultural scripts complement those of the families in your classroom? How do your communications highlight similarities in cultural scripts? How do your communications highlight differences in cultural scripts? How are similarities or differences in cultural scripts and communication reflected within the classroom environment?

Culturally competent communication means that we understand our own contributions to communication, the contributions of others, and the interaction between the two. Let's revisit the teachers and family in the opening vignette and look more closely at the skills needed to support cultural competency.

Although Mary Irene and Josie explained the purpose of the ASQ to the family, outlined the process, and discussed the various outcomes of screening before they asked the family to complete the instrument, the teachers did not anticipate the family's reaction. For the teachers, the benefits of early intervention are clear: if a child scores low on the ASQ screening, the natural outcome is communication with the pediatrician and a more formal assessment to see if early intervention is needed.

To Aidan's parents, a low score in the communication domain means very little. They are nervous about bringing a concern to their pediatrician, and early intervention sounds like a challenge they do not have the resources for right now. The teachers feel they have communicated in a language that is easy to understand; however, Aidan's parents do not really understand why they filled out the ASQ in the first place, why the teachers are concerned, and what the teachers are outlining as next steps. Aidan's parents understand the words, but the meaning behind them is lost. They are receiving a message that the situation is not good and that it is potentially something they have caused. Further, Aidan's father recently lost his job, and the family is struggling to pay their monthly bills. Beyond the cost of seeing the doctor, is early intervention expensive? How could they possibly pay for it? If they just wait, won't Aidan just start communicating on his own?

ISSUES OF OPPORTUNITY: SUPPORTING DUAL LANGUAGE LEARNERS

Often, families who are learning English worry that speaking their home language with their child will interfere with the child's ability to learn a new language. Research has demonstrated that there are many benefits for children in maintaining their home language, and families play a critical role in ensuring that this happens. Professionals can support families in fulfilling this role.

Families may have varied reactions to maintaining the home language. While some may view this as important, others might be concerned that maintaining the home language will interfere with the child's acculturation and future social and academic success. Use your active listening skills to carefully identify family concerns. From that point, use your joining and supporting skills with the goal of building consensus; informing families that the development of two languages benefits children's language, memory, and attention; and reassuring them that learning two languages will not delay a child's acquisition of English.

What can teachers do to ensure families are supported? Consider the following:

Send curriculum materials home in the child's home language.

Create as much continuity as possible between languages in the home and school environment.

Display family photos around the classroom, and learn key words in the child's language.

Support family literacy skills in their home language and English by connecting them with community literacy organizations.

Part of the challenge outlined in the vignette centers on the miscommunication that is occurring between the teachers and Aidan's parents. Each group understands the words that the others are using, but the language codes (ASQ, screening, early intervention) and contextual meanings of each group are not being communicated. Although each group is communicating with the other, they are misreading the deeper messages that are shaping communication. Mary Irene and Josie need to develop cultural competence, where they learn more about how culture is affecting the messages they are trying to convey as well as learn how the family's culture is shaping their response.

Defining Culturally Competent Communication

A competent communicator is appropriate and effective. She has mastery of a variety of different skills:

> when to make eye contact,
>
> when to use gestures, and which gestures are appropriate,
>
> appropriate use of volume and pitch,
>
> the right amount of space to give people,
>
> when to use tactile cues, such as pats on the back,
>
> how to orient her body,
>
> appropriate posture, and
>
> appropriate facial expressions.

A *culturally* competent communicator knows how to communicate within a particular cultural context (Wang, 2011). Cultural competence requires, for example, knowing when to make direct eye contact, preferences for looking down and away, when to use a handshake greeting as a hello, and when not to. Cultural competence requires merging context and knowledge, which shapes the decision-making process for effective communication.

How do you gather all of this information? You have at your disposal one of the most effective research tools you could possibly use—the power of observation! Carefully watch people as they interact with you. What seems to make them comfortable? Do you pick up on any actions you engage in that seem to cause discomfort? What conclusions might you draw from this? Remember that you want to avoid drawing broad generalizations based on such aspects as gender or ethnicity. Rather, follow the cues of others, watch their reactions, and develop your own personalized schemas—base your responses and interactions on that specific family. Develop skills in following someone else's lead: while I might hold out my hand when meeting someone, in some situations I might hold back and follow the other person's lead. Part of being a culturally competent communicator is based on being mindful, using focus and attention.

COMMUNICATION TIPS

Gestures are not universal, and their use may cause unnecessary miscommunication. For example, consider the two-finger *V* sign. In the United States, this gesture means *peace,* while in Australia the meaning is very derogatory. The thumbs-up sign in the United States generally means that all is going well; however, in Islamic and Asian countries, this gesture is considered rude and offensive.

Different cultures have different concepts of appropriate personal space. In Western cultures, acceptable personal space is generally two to four feet. In Latin American or Middle Eastern cultures, acceptable personal space is one to three feet; touching during conversations is common.

In the United States, maintaining eye contact is encouraged. In many other cultures, direct eye contact is a sign of disrespect.

These concepts can guide you, but this information cannot replace what you will learn through interaction with individuals. Researcher Carol Long identified additional skills related to cultural competency. Here, they are adapted to the field of early childhood education:

Demonstrate respect by assessing the family's primary language and dialect.

Determine language, dialect, and English proficiency, and secure an interpreter if needed. Make sure that you are communicating with the key players in the child's life. Use active listening, seeking, and verifying skills to ensure that you understand the family's perspective. Understanding their meaning is a precursor to your successful communication.

Be present and "join the journey" by connecting with a family's stories, goals, and dreams for their child. Keep in mind that their perspective in terms of temporal relationships and schemas might differ greatly from your own. Your ability to communicate will be affected by your ability to understand their world relative to their child.

Demonstrate respect and dignity. Assess and respond to nonverbal communication, including time orientation, body language, spatial distance/boundaries, touch, and eye contact. Observation will be essential, and mindfully following the family's cues will affect communication.

Be open to the process of communication. Communication is bidirectional—learn to adjust based on feedback and new directions that emerge in conversations.

DIFFERING PERSPECTIVES ON DISABILITY

How are a child's varying abilities perceived? Effective communication requires being aware of your perceptions, and in turn, of how your perceptions influence your communication.

A close friend, for example, has a young daughter who has Down syndrome. Their family believes that they were chosen by God to raise this little girl. I, on the other hand, believe that my daughter's genetic disorder that resulted in muscular dystrophy is something that just happened and just is. In both of our cases, there is a genetic disorder but a difference in the underlying belief system. Neither set of beliefs is right or wrong, but each is what we hold to be true.

An early childhood educator working with one of our children might have a belief system that complements one of the systems outlined above or one that is completely different. Challenges in communication can occur if an individual imposes her belief system on another or tries to convince someone else of the merits of holding a different position. These challenges are compounded when belief systems are unconscious and the person is unaware of how personal beliefs are affecting attitudes and interactions. For example, an educator might comment to a parent that her child is one of "God's little angels." This comment is reflective of the educator's belief system but may not be reflective of the parents'.

Learn about and respect a family's belief system, and work to understand how these beliefs affect their interaction with their child. From this vantage point, effective communication and collaboration can occur.

Building Relationships in the Context of Culturally Competent Communication

Our cultural frameworks provide us with unique cultural scripts for viewing, processing, and interacting with our worlds. The cultural scripts we carry serve as tools that guide us in solving human problems. Effective communication requires learning about another individual's cultural scripts. In your role as an early childhood educator, this includes learning about a family's strengths, concerns, priorities, and resources relative to their child. For Mary Irene and Josie in the vignette, effective communication would include learning what Aidan's family does know about screening, assessment, and early intervention; why they are feeling overwhelmed; and what kinds of resources the family might find beneficial. They can gather this information by using an approach developed by Antonella Surbone and Walter Baile: BALANCE—beliefs and values, ambience, language and literacy, affiliations, network, challenges, and economics (see Table 4.2).

TABLE 4.2: THE BALANCE APPROACH	
Beliefs and values	What does the family believe? For Aidan's family, what are their current beliefs regarding Aidan's development? Do they have any concerns? What are their overall goals?
Ambience	What is the family's structure and living situation? For Aidan's family, what kinds of supports do they have in place for Aidan within the home? What factors within the home environment do they find supportive? What factors do they find stressful?
Language and literacy	Is there a role for interpreters or need for translation? What language and literacy considerations are there?
Affiliations	What are the family's community ties? For Aidan's family, do they have organizations and groups they belong to that are beneficial? Are there other children and families in their lives?
Network	What is the family's social support system? For Aidan's family, is there a strong, supportive network? Might the early childhood environment play a larger role in being part of a supportive network?
Challenges	What current challenges is the family facing in terms of home, work, and life conditions? For Aidan's family, how is the father's current work situation affecting the family overall? How might this affect their access to resources?
Economics	What are the family's socioeconomic and community resources? For Aidan's family, what additional resources might they benefit from in their current situation?

Use the BALANCE approach in gathering meaningful information about a family. This data will provide you with information that goes beyond a surface exchange and that you can use to understand the family's and child's interests, needs, and strengths:

What are the interests, needs, and strengths that could link the child and family with a wider network of supports?

What are the family's current strengths in managing their daily lives and meeting their child's needs? How can these strengths be expanded?

What would the family like to do to support their child's development and learning?

What is the family's approach to problem solving?

What are the family's concerns, hopes, and plans?

(Adapted from Turnbull and Summers, 1987.)

Gathering information from families requires developing skills. Another strategy is called the RESPECT model: rapport, empathy, support, partnership, explanations, cultural competence, and trust. Originally developed for use within medical care, it is adapted in Table 4.3 for early childhood professionals.

TABLE 4.3: THE RESPECT MODEL	
Rapport	Connect on a social level. Work to suspend judgment. Recognize and avoid making assumptions.
Empathy	Seek to understand the family member's point of view on issues related to child rearing. Verbally acknowledge and legitimize the family member's perspective.
Support	Involve other family members as appropriate. Reassure the family that your goal is to develop a partnership. Connect with community resources as needed.
Partnership	Allow mutual control in communication exchanges. Negotiate roles. Stress that you are working together.
Explanations	Check often for understanding, both of messages sent and of those received. Use verbal clarification techniques.
Cultural competence	Respect the family member and her cultural beliefs. Understand that the family's view of you might be shaped by their own individual stereotypes. Be aware of your own biases and preconceptions.
Trust	Take the time to work with the family to ensure that a trusting relationship is developed.
(Adapted from Mutha, Allen, and Welch, 2002.)	

Mary Irene and Josie decide to apply the RESPECT model in their work with Aidan's family. Their first step in establishing rapport is to move beyond their initial perceptions of the family's reaction and to work to establish a connection where they were each open to what the parents have to say. They carefully listen and work hard to understand the parents' point of view. Their practice of empathy as they listen reassures the McMahans that they are respected. The parents reveal that the family did not understand the assessment or early intervention process, were concerned the pediatrician would judge them, and were worried about their ability to pay for services. Based on this new knowledge, the teachers are able to offer appropriate support: additional information about the process, an explanation of the benefits of seeking the pediatrician's advice and of early intervention, and potential monetary supports. The teachers' and family's shared understanding contributes to the development of an effective partnership. Throughout the process, Mary Irene and Josie ask questions both to make sure they understand the parents and the parents understand them. The explanations that each provide to the other contributes to a new, shared understanding. The entire process contributes to the development of their cultural competence. The time they take to work with the family and understand their perspective contributes to the development of trust, which serves as a basis for their ongoing relationship.

Applying the RESPECT model allows Mary Irene and Josie to learn about their own contributions to the communication exchange and provides an opportunity for them to learn about Aidan's family's contributions.

Chapter Reflection Questions

What are some of your cultural scripts regarding the care and education of young children? Think about these scripts as they specifically relate to feeding, nap time, guidance, and the role of play.

What are your preferred modes of communication with family members in your early childhood environment?

In what ways do you demonstrate respect for a family's preferred mode of communication?

What strategies do you use to learn about a family's cultural scripts?

Questions to Explore with Families

What are some of the family's cultural scripts regarding parenting? Consider scripts as they specifically relate to feeding, nap time, guidance, and the role of play.

What are the family's preferred modes of communication?

What are their interests, needs, and strengths?

What do they see as their current strengths in terms of their daily lives and meeting their child's needs?

What would they like to learn more about to support their child's development and learning?

What strategies do they use to solve problems?

What are their concerns, hopes, and plans for their child?

Culturally and Linguistically Competent Organizations

CHAPTER 5

Leticia has been the director at a NAEYC-accredited community early childhood program for several years. She is proud of the many strengths of their program. Her staff is wonderful at developing appropriate, engaging activities that support the development and learning of each child. Their center environment is welcoming and alive with learning.

Engaging the families in the program has been a challenge for Leticia and the staff. They plan activities, including family nights and opportunities to volunteer in the classroom, but only a small percentage of families choose to become involved. Over the past year, Leticia and the program's assistant director have attended training opportunities focused on developing cultural competency within their organization. They have learned strategies to create an engaging program and classroom communities. Despite their work in this area, Leticia is not sure that their program truly engages the families. Wanting to address the challenge, Leticia wonders where to begin. How can she create a culturally and linguistically responsive program that supports each family?

Building Culturally and Linguistically Responsive Organizations

As early childhood organizations become increasingly diverse, staff need to look at how to engage families in a comprehensive, systematic way that is respectful and responsive to each family's needs. Your ability to communicate with families in a culturally competent way is an important precursor to engagement. Couple your individual efforts with organizationally competent practices. Consider, for example, a family who is invited to join in classroom and program activities but has no opportunity to give input into the kinds of activities that occur and receives no guidance as to how they might participate. The family has access, but their participation is limited because they are not supported in their potential role. To support family access and full participation, staff and organizations need to work seamlessly together to create engaging environments.

In addition to cultural competence, linguistic competence is also important. Linguistically competent organizations and individuals share information in a way that is easily understood by varied audiences, including persons of limited English proficiency, those who have low literacy skills, individuals who have varying abilities, and persons who are deaf or hard of hearing. Imagine a teacher who uses words in a family's home language for daily communication. The larger program, however, provides center newsletters and other forms of communication only in English; consequently, the family is often unaware of larger program events. Communicating solely in English limits the family's full access and participation. The lack of systematic, comprehensive culturally and linguistically competent practices at the organizational level has a direct impact on family access and participation.

Just as we each have unique personal social identities, organizations also have identities. Each organization develops a unique cultural framework, which may welcome and encourage diversity or may demand conformity. Just as we need to be in touch with our social identities and how these influence our cultural framework, organizations that want to be culturally and linguistically competent need to consider these factors at an institutional level.

Engaging families within organizations requires that each family has access and can fully participate and that staff and families have needed supports to function optimally.

Optimal supports can mean different things—a family might need information on child development or community services, while a staff member might need information on culturally responsive teaching practices. Responsive organizations are flexible and fluidly meet varied needs.

Ensuring each family has access and can participate, and that families and staff have needed supports, requires attention to cultural competence. Culturally competent organizations respond to the unique social identities of the individuals within the organization, allowing each member to develop and thrive. NAEYC's Quality Benchmark for Cultural Competence Project (2009) outlines seven concepts that define cultural competence within early childhood organizations:

Acknowledge that children and families are nested in families and communities, and that these families and communities have unique strengths.

Build on and support the shared strengths, goals, and commonalities of the early childhood field and families.

Work to understand and meaningfully incorporate the traditions and history of program participants and their influence on child-rearing practices.

Support each child's development within the family, respecting complex and culturally driven ongoing experiences.

Recognize and demonstrate awareness that the practices of individuals and institutions are deeply rooted in culture.

Ensure that program decisions and policies respect and embrace participant language, values, attitudes, beliefs, and approaches to learning.

Ensure that program practices and policies build on the dialects and home languages of children, families, and staff, and that the program respects the preservation of home languages.

WHO ARE WE AS AN ORGANIZATION?

Ask three of your coworkers the following questions:

What do you think is most important to our early childhood organization?

What do you think are the main goals of our organization?

If you had to identify two factors that summarize what we are all about as a program, what would these factors be?

After you collect the responses of your coworkers, add your own responses to these questions. What did you learn about your program? How closely do you feel the perspectives you gathered align with what the program states are the overall goals? How do you feel these perspectives reflect what you feel an ideal program's overall goals would be?

These concepts were developed as part of a national effort to provide guidance for states in assessing cultural competence within Quality Rating Improvement Systems (QRIS). QRIS can play an important role in developing cultural and linguistic competence at the organizational level.

Exploring Organizational Culture and Identity

Organizations have an identity that responds to the question "Who are we?" *We* might represent a program that provides high-quality care and education services, a high-quality inclusive program, or a high-quality inclusive program that is culturally and linguistically responsive and works to engage each family. Organizational culture and identity are closely connected. Culture is the assumptions, beliefs, and values that people use to define who they are relative to the larger identity of the organization. Any organization can have multiple cultures within it (Albert and Whetten, 1985). For example, teachers might have one sense of identity relative to their work, while administrators might have another sense of identity.

Leticia, from our opening vignette, wants to learn more about the identity of her early childhood program. She feels her program has focused on developmentally appropriate practices and that they have many existing strengths: commitment to including families in daily activities, daily communication with families using both written and verbal strategies, reflection of the daily lives of children and families in pictures and books throughout the classroom environment, and use of words in each family's home language. But, Leticia wants to do more to develop an identity as a culturally and linguistically competent program. Both she and the staff want family engagement to be a central aspect of this identity.

Within any early childhood program, there are rich differences that either can be celebrated and used as tools to increase connection and understanding or ignored and used as catalysts to promote disengagement and discouragement. When a program manages the differences, access and full participation are supported. Organizations can carefully recognize and value differences among individuals in a number of areas:

> experiences,
>
> perceptions,
>
> ways of communicating and interacting,
>
> goals, and
>
> expected outcomes.

Creating a respectful, reciprocal, and responsive program means that you cannot make changes to the program alone. Develop a leadership team that values the diversity of staff and families served, and work together to create your space and place.

Developing a Diverse Leadership Team and Governance Structure

Decisions in early childhood programs are often made in a top-down fashion that limits cultural competency. A more effective approach includes creating a diverse leadership team of individuals who can help make decisions that are informed by their own personal experiences. This requires opening the membership of the leadership team to reflect the individual identities of the people who comprise the organization's identity; providing all members with an orientation about the goals of the leadership team; and gathering information from the team members about what topics are most important to them.

Families must have meaningful input, as well, into all aspects of program planning and decision making. Expand board membership by offering slots for family members, and provide opportunities for family members to participate in curriculum and financing teams and committees. Program leadership should reflect the identities of the people affected.

Changes to the leadership structure can create the potential for increased cultural competency and changes in the culture of the organization: if families are seen in leadership roles, this sends the message that family input is valued.

Addressing Hiring Policies

Staff within early childhood programs meet licensing requirements, and many meet additional requirements outlined by QRIS and accrediting bodies. A workforce that is responsive to child and family diversity requires hiring people who reflect the races, language backgrounds, and communities of the young children and families being served. The NAEYC Quality Benchmark for Cultural Competence Tool (2009) specifically recommends that if 20 percent of the children in the program speak a language other than English, a staff person should be hired who speaks that language.

Hiring policies that are culturally and linguistically competent foster a strong sense of identity for children who are racially and ethnically diverse, support children in the development of both their home language and their English skills, and encourage family engagement with the early childhood environment.

Including family members as decision makers in the program and changing hiring practices are important steps in increasing a program's cultural and linguistic competence; however, placing someone within a role does not mean that person is fully prepared to function within the role—access does not ensure participation. To support full participation, address professional and family education practices in a comprehensive and systematic way.

Meeting Professional and Family Education Needs

What are the components of culturally competent professional and family education? According to the National Black Child Development Institute, family education needs to move beyond an expert-learner relationship—where early childhood professionals are considered the experts and families the learners—to a model that encourages families to apply child development knowledge to their own needs. This model recognizes the knowledge families already have, which is a cornerstone of culturally competent professional and family education. The early childhood professional is a source of knowledge for educational theory and pedagogy, while the family is a central source of knowledge for information about the child.

Family engagement in early childhood environments is enhanced when families have a better understanding of the work professionals do and why they do it. Family educational activities must support and enhance family knowledge of educational theory and pedagogy used by program staff (NAEYC, 2009). To do this, programs need to

give families information about what is happening within early childhood classrooms;

clearly explain why things are happening;

identify how practices are supporting children's development and learning; and

outline connections to the family's role.

Family education activities can also increase the family's active participation by increasing their comfort with the early childhood environment. Offer classroom orientation and information on how families can meaningfully engage in the program. Provide families with an overview of the schedule; give families an outline of daily activities and what happens during each activity; and offer specific information on how they can get actively involved.

Many families have experienced barriers to engagement in the past. Some families have had negative experiences in educational systems early on, and these previous messages can strongly affect their participation. A few families do not recognize that their participation in their child's education is important, and others lack transportation and child care. Addressing challenges requires tackling both obstacles as well as educating families about the importance of their role.

To move family involvement forward, consider:

surveying families about past experiences;

addressing structural obstacles to family engagement in program activities by providing food, child care, transportation, and so on; and

developing marketing materials that communicate the values and positive outcomes of family engagement.

Some families might have specific needs when it comes to family education. For example, some families may have children who qualify for special education services, but the family members may not fully understand their legal rights and the rights of their children and may be unfamiliar with legal mandates and processes. Consider developing programming to educate all families about their rights and their role in their child's education. Include information about identification, referral, and intervention processes as well as legal, ethical, and financial matters (Al-Hassan and Gardner, 2002).

Families and staff may also have differing levels of comfort regarding their understanding of Individualized Family Service Plans (IFSPs) and Individualized Education Programs (IEPs). Some families may be overwhelmed about their specific role, and some teachers may be unsure of how to involve families in daily instruction. Consider including educational activities for families and professionals that clearly outline their roles in the development and implementation of the IFSP or IEP.

Culturally competent communication requires a breadth of knowledge and a range of skills. Consider the following education supports for staff:

training on communication with diverse families, including translation, interpretation, and use of cultural mediators;

training on understanding the cultural practices of the populations served;

tips for how to engage families in culturally sensitive ways;

ideas on supporting second-language acquisition;

training on local cultures and culturally based definitions of child development and early childhood education;

exploring cultural influences on their own practices and beliefs;

training on culturally competent communication practices; and

exploring cross-cultural issues in child-rearing practices.

Tending to family and professional education needs is likely to have an overall effect on both the identity and culture of the organization. As families and professionals become increasingly in tune with each other's perspectives, the answer to "Who are we?" will broaden. Changes to the culture come with increased awareness of other perspectives as well. As your schema expands to include new ways of understanding how others view the world, your interactions will alter and deepen.

Utilizing Family Conferences

Family conferences are an opportunity to provide information on children's growth and development, to address any concerns or questions that the family might have, and for staff to share any of their concerns. Conferences are also an opportunity for gathering meaningful information from families based on a shared understanding of the child. Responsiveness allows for connection and synergy; family and staff together explore culturally based understandings of child goals, strengths, and challenges (NAEYC, 2009). Teachers might have more knowledge in the areas of child development, academic settings, and requirements, but the family has unique knowledge of the child's experiences and skills. Both sets of knowledge are essential to supporting development and learning (Barrera, Corso, and Macpherson, 2003).

TIPS FOR CONDUCTING EFFECTIVE FAMILY CONFERENCES

Survey the family prior to the conference to determine the kinds of information they would like to learn and what they would like to share.

Include in your communication the information you plan on sharing.

Provide several dates and times to choose from for the conference.

Off-site locations might be more convenient for some families, so consider community locations as an alternative to on-site meetings.

Send reminders for the event.

If a translator is needed, have someone available.

Provide child care.

Be organized.

Have everything prepared in the family's preferred communication format.

Carefully gather information about the family's strengths, concerns, priorities, and resources.

Be mindful, and use your active listening skills.

Thoroughly address each question the family has.

Develop goals and an action plan together.

Determine a follow-up plan.

Allow adequate time between conferences in case the conference runs over.

Follow up with the family, addressing any questions they may have had.

Communicate about your shared goals and action plan.

Keep the lines of communication open.

Consider your overall goals for the conference. Work with the family to set goals for the child and to create a method for monitoring and supporting the progress made toward these goals:

Work collaboratively with the family to foster high expectations for achievement.

Show the family what their child is learning, and explain how this aligns with age-level expectations.

Offer suggestions for ways the family can support the child's learning at home (Speilberg, 2011).

Widening Program Communication with Families

How a program communicates with families strongly affects the families' perceptions of the program. Family conferences are one formal form of communication within programs. Programs can also have a variety of other formal and informal methods of communication.

Your ability to successfully communicate is based on your ability to understand your schemas and their effect on the unique social identities and schemas of others. At an individual and organizational level, this can communicate that you value individuality and diversity. Organizations demonstrate a value for diversity through effective, respectful communication strategies tailored to each family's preferred styles of communication. Often, families are asked about their preferred modes of communication on program enrollment forms. While many families are comfortable and confident in filling out the forms, not all families feel comfortable with this process. Families vary in cultural styles of communication, language use, and anxiety levels related to language and to school organizations, as well as reading levels. Each of these issues, as well as others, can interfere with a family's responses. Gather information about communication preferences in a variety of ways, both written and verbal. If language or reading ability is an issue, consider giving families pictorial representations of different communication strategies they can choose from. For example, if your program provides newsletters, emails, phone calls, video clips, and face-to-face communication as regular communication strategies, including small icons that represent each of these options next to the word can help promote family understanding. Remember to ask families regularly how they feel communication is going and what you can do to foster better communication. This process is outlined in Figure 5.1.

FIGURE 5.1: REVISITING COMMUNICATION STRATEGIES

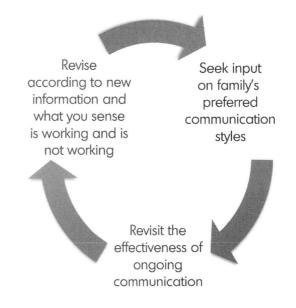

Revise according to new information and what you sense is working and is not working

Seek input on family's preferred communication styles

Revisit the effectiveness of ongoing communication

USING INTERPRETERS

Interpreters have a challenging job: they must fully understand the context and cultural meaning of both languages in order for successful communication to take place. Without careful attention to each of these factors, many miscommunications can arise.

Effective interpreters must have a variety of skills:

linguistic competencies in the first and second language;

cultural competencies that support understanding of varied meanings in both first and second language; and

ethical and professional standards of confidentiality, neutrality, collaboration, and interpersonal communication (Lynch and Hanson, 2004).

According to the National Center for Cultural Competence, cost, time, and lack of knowledge of how to work with interpreters can leave many programs relying on untrained interpreters, including family and friends and bilingual staff. Community interpreter banks, where costs are shared among partners, participants, or customers, can be a cost-effective way to provide a wide range of languages to a community. Learn about the interpreter resources available in your community.

Take a look at your program's communication practices: When and how does the program communicate? Are communications typically from the program to the families, but not from the families to the program? Does the program use a variety of communication strategies? If a family has access to a computer and email, electronic newsletters, blogs, websites, emails, photos, and video clips can keep them up-to-date on information, upcoming events, concerns, or issues. The family can also use email to communicate with the caregiver quickly, easily, and privately. For families who do not have computer access, printed newsletters in their home languages can keep them up-to-date on general information and upcoming events. For private matters, telephone or face-to-face conversations can work well. Strive to communicate with each family in their preferred methods and in their home languages, using interpreters and translators where necessary.

Within any program, it is important to brainstorm potential situations where interpreter services can be used and to place this information in the policies and procedures manual. Using a variety of communication strategies helps break down a common barrier to engagement: a lack of information. Families need frequent and specific information about their child's progress. Providing information in a family's home language might not be sufficient, as some families might not be fully literate in their home language, which can further contribute to communication challenges. Consider requiring that all important information be provided in a variety of formats, including verbally and via audio translations, to increase accessibility.

Solicit feedback from families. Effective communication requires bidirectionality: you cannot state that communication has occurred if you do not know for sure that what you have communicated was understood. This means that families need opportunities to give feedback on the quality of communication.

Many organizations collect information on preferred modes of family communication at the beginning of the year. A family might indicate that they have several preferences for communication, including newsletters, email, and face-to-face conversations. As the school year progresses, those modes of communication may not meet their expectations or needs. Family situations may change, making a previously acceptable form of communication no longer feasible. To keep abreast of changing family needs, regularly assess each family's satisfaction with the ways the staff are communicating and the methods being used. This can be accomplished through formal surveys and informal conversations, whichever methods have proven to be most effective based on each family's preferences and needs.

You may think you know what information families are most interested in knowing about; however, family interests may or may not be in sync with the list your program has created. Further, family interests might vary throughout the year and from one year to the next. Consider surveying families semi-annually on the kinds of information they would like to have and how the program can individualize information based on family preferences.

Developing Community Outreach

Families represent a common thread across the early childhood classroom environment and the larger community. Respectful, reciprocal, and responsive organizations ensure each family's relationships are enhanced across each context. The relationship between family and community is bidirectional: families affect and are affected by their communities. Relationships you have with the community can strengthen relationships you have with the families you serve. Incorporating this information into early childhood organizations can serve to further engage families.

Establishing supportive relationships with the community is one of the central components of family engagement identified by Halgunseth et al. (2009). Building relationships and institutionalizing information begins with learning more about the community. Consider the following:

What languages are spoken in the community?

What are economic challenges affecting the community?

What are the community's strengths?

What is the community's overall view of education?

How might the community's beliefs about education affect how the early childhood program is viewed?

What insights can this information provide into supporting continuity between program and classroom practices and community beliefs, strengths, and challenges?

For example, consider what we know about young children and their families who are growing up in areas of concentrated poverty. In these communities, families are more likely to struggle to meet their children's basic material needs and are more likely to face food hardship and difficulties paying their housing costs. These children are also more likely to lack health insurance and to experience harmful levels of stress (Kids Count, 2012). An early childhood program for this community would have the potential to serve as an important resource and support.

How can you gather information about the community you serve? One strategy is to enlist key community informants, people who know and can share about the life of the community. Gather this information through interviews, informal and formal information-gathering sessions, and direct consultation provided to the program (National Center for Cultural Competence).

Another strategy is enlisting cultural brokers. *Cultural brokers* are individuals who serve as bridging, mediating, or linking agents between different cultural groups for the purpose of reducing conflict or producing change (Jezewski, 1990). Cultural brokers can help community members understand the benefits of high-quality care and education, explain the benefits of family engagement within a program, and ease participation in program services. Cultural brokers can help programs identify and understand obstacles families perceive in becoming involved in the early childhood program.

Focus groups can provide a program with information about community perceptions of the role of early childhood education as well as factors that might affect families within the community, including domestic violence, unemployment rates, working and housing conditions, transportation and economic challenges, and community demographics (National Center for Cultural Competence).

LOOKING THROUGH YOUR CULTURAL LENS: SERVING AS A CULTURAL BROKER

The field of early childhood education represents its own culture, in which core values are built into policies and practices. One of the core values stressed in family engagement is creating a culture that allows families to share with professionals in the decision-making process of their child's education. Families, however, might not share that core value or might not be fully prepared to participate within a culture that they know little about. Early childhood teachers are in a unique role as cultural brokers who can provide information about the field, its practices, and its outcomes to those who are unfamiliar with it. Effective cultural brokers are knowledgeable about their own culture and have the ability to communicate that knowledge to others.

The early childhood field uses a specific language, a set of practices, and ways of supporting young children's development and learning. Self-reflection about your own value system and how it aligns with practices in early childhood education is a great first step in exploring the field as a culture. How does knowledge in the field match your own beliefs about child development and learning? Which practices do you feel most align with your belief system? Which practices do you feel differ most from your belief system? How might the information you share with families align with their belief systems?

Family wisdom and values may differ from the cultural practices in early childhood education. Our ability to truly communicate and collaborate with families about different perspectives requires that we are able to see that we have a lens and are able to serve as a broker to explain this lens to others.

Leticia and her leadership team, from our opening vignette, conduct focus groups in their community and learn that literacy is an issue. Based on this information, they decide to sponsor family-child reading activities and to partner with local libraries to ensure children have books in their homes.

Family participation rates are low, as well. Leticia and the team learn that the community lacks an awareness of the benefits of high-quality early childhood education programs. So, they decide to conduct community-based activities designed to support child development, increase program awareness, and educate families about the benefits of high-quality early childhood education.

Integrating the community into the program requires attention to program structure—how might members of the community give input into the early childhood program? To further integrate the community into the program, consider creating spots for community members on advisory boards, task forces, and committees to elicit input and expertise into program planning, design, and implementation. Ensure the program practices complement and support the needs of the existing community (National Center for Cultural Competence).

Keep in mind that the general strengths and challenges faced by individuals in each community do not always reflect the realities of all community members. There is danger to overgeneralizing or stereotyping, based on the misconception that all members of a community are similar to one another. Taking the time to learn about the community is respectful to both the families and the community and is an important step in designing organizations and classrooms that support young children and their families. Through learning about the community and working to weave that community into the program and classroom in a variety of ways, the respectful foundation that has been established can blossom into a thriving relationship where classroom, program, family, and community become interdependent. As the family represents the common thread, a web of support for the family can be established from this interdependent relationship.

Your program's evolution will not be static, and your goals of developing cultural and linguistic competence as a tool to engage families will need to be monitored over time.

Conducting Ongoing Program Assessment

Developing a culturally responsive program is not a one-time event, where policies and practices are developed and allowed to grow stagnant. Ongoing assessment is an important part of the equation, as is the process of adaptation. Just as a child changes developmentally, organizations change over time with the staff employed, children and families enrolled, challenges faced, and overall strengths.

CULTURAL COMPETENCE SELF-ASSESSMENT

1. Is your program able to describe the strengths of the families served?

   ○ Yes   ○ No

2. Is your program able to identify priorities of the families served?

   ○ Yes   ○ No

3. Is your program able to identify concerns of the families served?

   ○ Yes   ○ No

4. Is your program able to identify the support networks and resources of families served?

   ○ Yes   ○ No

5. Is your program able to describe the languages and dialects used by the families served?

   ○ Yes   ○ No

6. Is your program aware of families' child-rearing beliefs regarding feeding, sleeping, eating, communication, discipline, exploring and learning, and fostering independence?

   ○ Yes   ○ No

7. Is your program aware of families' customs and values?

   ○ Yes   ○ No

8. For questions 1 through 7, does your center have a policy supporting staff training in community cultural beliefs and practices?

   ○   No   ○ Informal policy   ○ Formal policy

9. Does your program have a policy encouraging shared decision making among families and professionals to establish mutually agreed-upon goals and to develop resources, supports, and services?

   ○   No   ○ Informal policy   ○ Formal policy

10. Does your program include a policy supporting families and professionals working as team members in planning, delivering, and evaluating early intervention and early childhood special education services?

    ○   No   ○ Informal policy   ○ Formal policy

11. Does your program have a mission statement that reflects cultural competence in service delivery?

    ○ Yes   ○ No

12. Does your program incorporate culture in service delivery?

    ○ Yes   ○ No

13. Does your program systematically review procedures to ensure that they reflect cultural competency?

    ○ Yes   ○ No

14. Does your program employ individuals who represent and are members of the cultures of the community you serve?

    ○ Yes   ○ No

15. Does your program employ linguistically diverse individuals?

    ○ Yes   ○ No

16. Does your program conduct in-service trainings on cultural competence?

    ○ Yes   ○ No

Chapter Reflection Questions

What is the current identity of your early childhood program? What do you see as your program's ideal identity?

What are current strengths and challenges in terms of how your leadership team and governance structure reflect families?

Do organizational hiring practices support diversity?

How do professional and family-education practices support family engagement needs?

What strategies are used during family conferences to support family engagement?

How do program communication strategies support family engagement?

How does the program use family history and traditions to inform program policies and practices?

In what ways does the program collaborate with the larger community?

In what ways does the program conduct ongoing assessment specific to family engagement practices?

Questions to Explore with Families

What do you see as the ideal components of a program that supports families?

What ways would you most like to become involved within the early childhood program?

❖ What do you see as obstacles to your involvement?

❖ What kinds of information would you like to share and have shared during a family conference?

❖ How would you like the program staff to communicate with you?

What aspects of your history and traditions do you feel are most important in terms of your child's functioning within the program?

❖ What connections would you most like to build with the larger community?

Culturally and Linguistically Competent Classrooms

CHAPTER 6

The staff at the Child Development Lab was thrilled to welcome the Diallo family to their early childhood program. The family included two-year-old Solange, four-year-old Grace, and the children's mother, father, and grandmother. The family had recently arrived from the Republic of the Congo. The father spoke a bit of English, and he and the rest of the family spoke French and Kituba.

Two-year-old Solange was welcomed into Linda and Stevie's infant and toddler classroom, and four-year-old Grace into Vickie and Joellen's mixed-age-group preschool environment. With a great deal of thought and reading about how to support the new arrivals, the teachers' planning for the girls and their family began long before the girls' first day in the classroom. One of the factors they needed to consider was that Solange had been diagnosed with cerebral palsy and would be receiving early intervention services both in her home and in the classroom.

The teachers explored several questions as they prepared: How could they best communicate with the family? What would help the girls and family feel most welcome? How could they support the girls' healthy growth and development? What goals were important to the family, and how could they work with them to support their goals?

Daily practices reflect identities and cultural frameworks. What you do to engage families on a day-to-day basis can make a huge difference in family access and participation. Imagine an environment where every family feels welcomed, every voice is heard, every person has a clear idea of what is happening within the program and classroom, and everyone's input is valued. Your attitude and the care and attention given to classroom and program practices can make the difference between families who feel respected, valued, and engaged and families who feel disempowered and devalued.

Foundations of Engaging Environments

Understanding your own social identities and how these influence your interactions with others is essential to creating an engaging environment. Additionally, you must get to know each family and put strategies in place that support partnership. The following are important strategies supporting family engagement:

conduct home visits,

create avenues for shared decision making,

create environments that welcome families, and

cultivate families as resources.

(Halgunseth et al., 2009)

Making sure your program and classroom truly engage families requires working from the outside in. Begin with understanding the family in their home.

Conducting Home Visits

Home visits are a wonderful way to get to know the social identities of families and establish relationships that can grow into effective partnerships. Extensive research indicates that a number of different home visiting models are effective in helping to develop thriving, mutual partnerships. Home visits are used extensively as a means of delivering early intervention services for young children between the ages of birth and two within natural environments.

Spending focused time with families away from busy classroom environments can be invaluable. These are times when you and the family can get to know each other. You can share a bit about who you are and learn who family members are. You can learn what they are like in their own homes and begin to learn what they value and perhaps what their dreams are for their children and themselves. Margery Ginsberg, in her article "Lessons at the Kitchen Table" in *Educational Leadership,* suggests questions to consider as you think about and plan home visits:

What can home visits teach us that might be hard to learn in another context?

What do we want to learn, with greater breadth and depth, about the lives of the children and families we serve?

How can we use what we learn to inform the relationships we are building, the children we are working with, and our teaching practices?

As teachers, how can home visits help dispel any assumptions we have and help us tune in to our own deficit thinking?

These questions explore ways home visits can provide information, lend insights, enhance teaching practices, and potentially strengthen relationships. Keep in mind that the reasons to conduct home visits and what happens during home visits are as individualized as the participants.

It is important to gather basic information prior to your first visit to a home. You can ask the family if they have communication preferences and if there are any rules in their home—such as taking shoes off at the door, entering through a preferred door, and so on—that they would like you to follow. Use open-ended questions to learn more about the family prior to your visit. Table 6.1 lists several standard, important components of home visits that exist despite the unique culture of each visit.

TABLE 6.1: COMPONENTS OF HOME VISITS

Component	Description
Planning	What is my purpose for this home visit? Is this child new to the classroom, or is the purpose of the visit ongoing communication and collaboration?
	What are my overall goals in terms of developing a partnership with this family?
	What steps can I take to best prepare the family for my home visit?
	What materials will I need to bring?
	What do I need to know about this family before I visit? For example, are there any cultural practices in their home that are important for me to follow? How can I gather this information in a culturally respectful way?
	What is the best way to communicate the reasons I am visiting their home and how long I would like to stay?
Greeting	What greeting is most appropriate for this family?
	What cues should I watch for to respect practices within their home—for example, taking off shoes, placement of coat, acceptance of beverage, and so on?
Activities	What will I do with the child and family while I am in their home?
	How do these activities complement my overall goals for the visit?
	How will I flexibly adapt my behavior and planned activities based on child and family needs?
Observation	What cues should I watch for to determine how comfortable the family and child are with me in their home?
	How will I adjust my behaviors based on the family's comfort level?
Sharing knowledge	What information do I want to share with the family while I am there?
	What do I want to share with the family about me?
	What information do I want to gather from the family during my visit?
	How does this information complement my overall goals for the visit?
Follow-up	How will I follow up with the family after my visit?
	How will I assess if the goals of my visit were appropriate and/or if they were achieved?
	What did I learn that did not necessarily align with my goals?
	Were my goals realistic?
	What steps should I take if my goals were not achieved?
(Adapted from Brorson, 2005.)	

THE POWER OF LISTENING TO FAMILY STORIES

Early childhood programs often use questionnaires to learn about new families. The questions are typically general in nature and can overlook the rich texture and unique aspects of individual lives. Digging deeper with the goal of understanding a family's social identity and communication style can, in turn, support cultural and linguistic continuity (Kidd, Sánchez, and Thorp, 2002).

Family stories provide a great opportunity to dig deeper! Through these stories, professionals can learn what factors such as language, race, ethnicity, religion, socioeconomic status, family structures, sexual orientation, and community mean to the family (Kaser and Short, 1998). Stories also provide an opportunity to learn what families value, their hopes and dreams, what motivates them, and their dilemmas (Sanchez, 1999). Stories can provide information about cultural frameworks that differ from our own, a true understanding of the families served, and how to design and implement culturally responsive teaching practices (Kidd, Sánchez, and Thorp, 2002).

Use prompts to help get the conversation started, such as the following:

"Tell me about Media's birth."

"Please share your story of coming to this country."

"What is your greatest source of joy in raising Lin?"

"What are some of the challenges you have experienced as a family?"

"What traditions are most important to you?"

There is great power in the request, "Tell me your story."

The Diallos' youngest daughter, Solange, receives early intervention services both in her home and at the Child Development Lab. During the home visits, an early intervention specialist demonstrates techniques that the Diallos can use to support their daughter's physical and language development.

The Diallos did not initially understand the purpose of these home visits. Their confusion reflects a common challenge in early intervention services: families often are expected to have professional knowledge, including understanding the meaning of a diagnosis and the services provided (Kalyanpur, Harry, and Skrtic, 2000). The teachers in Solange's classroom, with the help of a translator, communicated to the Diallos the role of early intervention services, the anticipated outcomes, and what would happen during each of

ISSUES OF OPPORTUNITY: INCLUSION

Research indicates that 50.9 percent of children with disabilities are being served in some kind of inclusive early childhood setting (U.S. Department of Education, 2010). The benefits of high-quality, inclusive programming for young children—with and without disabilities—and their families are extensive (Buysse, Goldman, and Skinner, 2002; Odom, 2002). The DEC/NAEYC Joint Position Statement on Inclusion (2009) reflects the commitment of national organizations working to support the development and learning of each child and establishes a shared national definition of inclusion.

Research indicates that the workforce is not fully prepared to support culturally, linguistically, and ability-diverse young children and families (Winton and McCollum, 2008). Practitioners must learn about each child's specific strengths and challenges and how to support that child. Caregivers can integrate information on best practices with their own knowledge and that gained by communicating with the family to determine the best ways to support the children's healthy development and learning. Collaboration among families, teachers and caregivers, and specialists is the key to high-quality inclusion (Hunt et al., 2004).

the home visits. The teachers also met with the therapist once a week in the classroom and talked to the Diallos about how they could embed Solange's therapies across her day. This information greatly increased the family's comfort and understanding of the early intervention home-visiting process.

Getting to know the family is essential to establishing respect, and home visits are a wonderful tool to use. Work to develop reciprocity as you seek family input and share in making decisions.

Creating Avenues for Shared Decision Making

Many programs have structures in place that create an avenue for family voices; policy councils within Head Start programs are a great example. Support access and full participation of all families in these opportunities (see Table 6.2). Some families might not feel confident. Others might not understand their child's educational needs. Some may have had previous negative experiences in the educational system. Some may experience structural obstacles such as a lack of transportation or child care. Each of these factors can affect participation.

TABLE 6.2: OPPORTUNITIES FOR FAMILY INPUT

Program Component	Information to Share	Opportunities for Input	Strategies
Curriculum	Program goals Information on early learning standards General plans for project and child-centered activities	Curriculum ideas Ideas for implementation and family involvement Extension ideas based on unique child and family situations	Make families aware of what is happening within the classroom. Solicit input into the curriculum. Solicit involvement with day-to-day activities. Provide a variety of opportunities for involvement: pouring juice; planting flowers in the play garden; sharing a favorite recipe, song, or story.
Policies and procedures manual	Program operations Program and classroom policies Implementation plans	Effects of policies and procedures Feedback on what works effectively for families Suggestions for revisions	Regularly survey families face-to-face, electronically, or on paper. Regularly ask for ideas for possible changes.
Staff development	Upcoming workshops Planned staff-development opportunities	Ideas for staff-development topics	Invite families to staff-development workshops. Give families opportunities to offer input into topic selection.
Family nights	Plans for family gatherings	Dates and times of events Topic selection	Survey families face-to-face, electronically, or on paper about event activities. Provide opportunities to share in event planning.
Building use	Organization and utilization of space	The effects of space use on families Feedback on space strengths and challenges Ideas on how space can be used differently	Regularly survey families face-to-face, electronically, or on paper about building use and ideas for change.

What strategies can you use to support access and participation? Access begins by giving families a voice. Think about your early childhood curriculum within your classroom: Where would family input be valuable? There are many aspects of every classroom where family input increases family and child engagement and supports positive child outcomes.

Creating opportunities for families to provide input does not mean they will participate! Understanding the challenges families may face can help you understand how to support participation. Keep in mind that each family has unique strengths and challenges regarding participation in shared decision making. One family might feel comfortable providing input and direction; another might need more direct coaching. Your role, then, is to create an environment that actively seeks to empower all families based on their individual strengths and challenges.

Communicate in a way that is understandable to families (see Table 6.3). Jargon and acronyms can add confusion to conversations. Asking families if they would like to give input into "activities children do during the day" is a more culturally neutral, conventional way to solicit involvement than "shared decision-making opportunities regarding curriculum."

TABLE 6.3: USING CONVENTIONAL LANGUAGE	
Instead of...	**Use the phrase...**
Cognitive development	Thinking skills
Gross motor area	Play area supporting large-muscle development
Developmentally appropriate practices	Practices that support a child's development and learning
Social and emotional development	How children feel about themselves and get along with others
Evidence-based practices	Practices based on research
Adaptations, modifications, and accommodations	Teaching practices supporting all children in the classroom environment
Literacy	Reading, writing, speaking, and listening skills

Consider, too, that a lack of involvement does not necessarily convey a lack of interest. Research indicates several aspects of families' economic and social circumstances that can contribute to low involvement, including a lack of transportation, lack of child care, a history of poor relationships with schools, and perceptions of their role within the school environment (Kalyanpur, Harry, and Skrtic, 2000).

Providing transportation and child care can alleviate the concerns of some families. For others, address distrust of institutions through ongoing communication that stresses respect, reciprocity, and responsiveness. For other families, clearly communicating that they have a valued role in the school environment and outlining what that role is can help address prior perceptions.

Successful participation requires that families know what is expected of them. Asking a family to attend a meeting to give input into family-night activities might seem like a concrete request, but families may have many questions. What will be expected of them at the meeting? Will they be expected to speak in front of people? Do they need to have prior knowledge? Is this an ongoing commitment? Requests need to be concrete, and families need specific information that will address their varied comfort levels.

Creating engaging, respectful, reciprocal, responsive environments requires including individuals from varied cultural, ethnic, and language backgrounds in the decision-making process. This process includes recognition that different groups might approach decision making differently and might have different viewpoints regarding endpoints and outcomes. Thinking through each of these factors when you invite people to the table is an important aspect of ensuring that the process is inclusive.

From our opening vignette, the Child Development Lab staff invited the Diallos and other families to various planning events. The staff was careful to make concrete requests and to overcome potential obstacles.

The Diallos became truly involved in the center when they made a specific request of the staff. About halfway through the year, Mr. Diallo told the center director, Megan, that many of his friends and associates were coming from the Republic of the Congo. He wanted to work with her on securing spots for their children in the lab school and on helping them with the transition. Megan welcomed both his ideas and his input, and together with a translator and a team of teachers, they worked to ensure that these new families would be engaged with the center.

The staff found that, after Mr. Diallo's involvement, the whole family's participation in other events increased. Megan's initial response to his particular area of interest was a key factor in soliciting their engagement. Creating avenues for shared decision making weaves family perspectives into the fabric of your program and creates a shared program identity.

Creating Environments That Welcome Families

Think about your favorite room in your home. What items in that environment are most comforting to you? Do you have favorite pictures, meaningful objects, and comfortable places to rest? How are your social identities reflected within that environment? What can you learn about your own preferences from your favorite room? What can others learn about you by viewing that environment?

The environments we encounter send different messages: A cold, stark environment might communicate that this is not a place to spend a great deal of time. A warm, inviting environment might communicate a welcoming feeling with the message "Stay a while. You belong here."

Early childhood environments may convey a general message: "This is a classroom that serves preschool-aged children." Or, these environments may convey a specific message: "This is a classroom that serves a unique group of preschool-aged children, whose appearance, homes, abilities, languages, and families may vary, but who share the bond of being in this community of learners."

What messages are important for families to receive from an early childhood environment? First and foremost, the environment needs to communicate that this is a place where every child and family belongs. This is a place that understands each family is a vital part of their child's early childhood environment. A learning space that engages families will welcome and honor their presence (Constantino, 2008). In addition to belonging, families need to know that they have a voice, that not only do they belong within the environment, but also that their input is valued and respected.

LOOKING THROUGH YOUR CULTURAL LENS: HOLIDAY CELEBRATIONS

The role of holiday celebrations in early childhood classrooms is a common debate in the field. We each may have holidays and rituals that we hold near and dear. If you are a member of the dominant culture, you might not think twice about extending those celebrations to the early childhood environment. For example, what harm is there in celebrating Valentine's Day, Christmas, or Halloween when the majority of children and families in America celebrate those holidays? If we look through the lens of family engagement, where we are trying to create access for all families and opportunities for meaningful participation, important questions arise:

Will the holiday alienate anyone within the environment and, therefore, work against creating a sense of belonging and acceptance?

How strongly do your own schemas shape your perception of the holiday? Is it possible, for example, that two individuals might view the historical significance of Thanksgiving differently and hold the celebration in differing lights?

Does a celebration based on your individual schema of the event reflect cultural competence?

Even if you identify all children and families in a classroom as practicing the same holidays, their rituals might differ from the ones you choose to include. Introducing holiday celebrations can also create challenges for some families. Having children pass out valentines to the entire class or dress up for Halloween, for example, might create a financial hardship.

One solution is to celebrate the holidays of all children and families within the classroom. Teachers in this situation must be mindful of creating meaningful celebrations that accurately reflect how children and families engage with the holiday. Another solution is to not celebrate specific holidays, but to infuse the core values of what is meaningful about the holiday into the classroom environment: the joy of getting together, sharing, or showing appreciation.

Socioeconomic factors can be addressed by carefully thinking through objectives and available resources. If the goal of exchanging valentines is showing appreciation, consider using materials in the classroom. If dressing up demonstrates creativity, consider using clothes in the dramatic play area. Supporting access and meaningful participation for each family requires thinking through the kinds of activities we design as well as the resources we provide.

Environments communicate a sense of belonging and respect through reciprocity and responsiveness (Barrera, Corso, and Macpherson, 2003). This requires far more than establishing an open-door policy and hoping that families will come to you with their ideas, concerns, hopes, and dreams. Rather, pay attention to how environments are designed. Consider the space created for families as well as the messages that the environment conveys.

Early childhood environmental design affects the individuals who spend time within the environment (Olds, 2001). Creating respectful environments for families begins with accommodating many kinds of communication. The space should include attention to comfort, places for families to sit and talk, and areas where small groups can gather and converse comfortably. Having a small sitting area arranged in the welcome area of the program supports gathering and communicating, while a small couch inside the classroom supports family communication with the teachers during drop-off and pickup times.

We often think of creating effective environments for families on an overt level, incorporating design strategies that are easily checked off a checklist. Looking carefully at what environments communicate beneath the surface—at the covert level—can tell us what the environment communicates to others about belonging and membership:

Is my family truly represented in this environment?

Is it OK for us to be ourselves here?

Do we truly belong?

When designing engaging environments, move beyond surface design strategies and include attention to deeper messages that support a sense of belonging and membership and truly support full inclusion. Reflect the rich identities of the families and staff through family photos, images of their homes, and pictures from their diverse communities. Provide written materials that are accessible to everyone, regardless of reading level and home language.

For the Diallos, photos of the girls and their family were displayed the first day the children entered their classrooms. The pictures included the family's previous home in the Republic of the Congo as well as their new home. The center made sure to provide books in the family's first language, French. The teachers worked hard to create a deep and clear message: "You truly belong here."

When you use images and other materials, make sure that they represent the families in an authentic way. For example, if you have a child in your class who is living with her two mothers, talk with the parents about whether or not to include a book in your classroom on growing up with two mothers. Consider asking them to help you choose materials that will be meaningful. If you have a child in your classroom whose family is from an Arabic culture, ask the family what traditions are most meaningful to them and how they can be incorporated in the classroom environment.

There are a number of resources on creating effective learning environments. A useful tool for creating environments for families is Universal Design (see Table 6.4), which is a paradigm that originated in architecture and stresses the design of buildings and products that are usable by all individuals, to the greatest extent possible, without adaptation or specialized design. When thinking about families, inclusive early childhood classrooms consider the following: How can the environment be accessible to all families served, ensure full participation and engagement, and communicate respect and welcome?

TABLE 6.4: CREATING ENGAGING FAMILY ENVIRONMENTS

Universal Design Principle	Description	Strategies for Access	Strategies for Participation
Equitable use	Design is useful to all families	Takes into account each family's language, culture, and abilities Materials available in home languages of families served Materials take into account literacy levels of families served	Families have space, such as a small sofa, for one-on-one conversations. Environment is equally appealing to all participants. Pictures posted within the environment reflect the homes, communities, and abilities of the children and families served.
Flexibility	Design accommodates a wide range of individual preferences and abilities	Information shared in a variety of formats: conversation, video, online, written, pictorial Information presented in languages and literacy levels that are accessible to all families	Families have a choice in how they participate within the environment: ❖ converse with teachers in the classroom ❖ conference in private ❖ meet with other families
Simple and intuitive use	Design is easy to understand, regardless of user's language skills, experience, knowledge, or concentration level	Signs are posted in a variety of different languages Signs incorporate pictures Signs account for variance in literacy levels	Families can enter the building or classroom environment and immediately know or intuit expectations. If families need assistance, it is apparent where to go for help.
Perceptible information	Environment communicates necessary information to the user, regardless of language skills, experience, knowledge, or concentration level	Information about building space, how to access materials, how to use the space, and how to get help if experiencing challenges is posted in languages reflected in environment, pictorially, and takes into account different literacy levels	

TABLE 6.4: CREATING ENGAGING FAMILY ENVIRONMENTS (continued)

Universal Design Principle	Description	Strategies for Access	Strategies for Participation
Tolerance for error	Design minimizes hazards and adverse consequence of accidents or unintended actions	Expectations at drop-off and transitions are clear The environment supports success When challenges do occur, guidance is readily available	
Low physical effort	Design can be used efficiently and comfortably with a minimum of fatigue		Comfortable places for families to gather Comfortable places for families to meet with staff Comfortable places for child drop-off and pickup Opportunities for communication not limited by design
Size and space for approach and use	Allows appropriate size and space for individuals, regardless of body size, posture, or mobility	Furnishings and accessories within the environment are selected to mirror the present family population Furniture and accessories are adjusted accordingly over time	

Creating engaging environments that are respectful of each family's identity sends the message that their presence is valued and supports access.

Even if they feel welcome in the classroom, some families may feel disconnected from the learning experiences of their children. Many experience barriers to involvement, such as work responsibilities and family stress. Barriers can inhibit a family's participation in the early childhood setting and their ability to learn about how to support their child (McWayne and Owsianik, 2004). You can help all families by recognizing and responding to barriers and providing well-designed home extension activities.

Home extension activities take into account family schedules and comfort levels and keep families informed about what is happening in your classroom. Effective extension activities complement a family's own knowledge, skills, and time constraints; include careful communication about why activities are important; and provide clear directions on how to complete the activity. Well-developed home extension activities help create a home-school connection and can provide families with a sense of empowerment about their essential role in their child's education.

The Diallo family is beginning to use home extension activities with Solange and Grace. The teachers have had the instructions translated into French for the family. So far, the family's favorite activity has been watching the flower seeds—provided by the preschool—growing in a cup on their windowsill at home.

Developing Families as Resources

Researchers have found that families' perspectives, wisdom, and knowledge are valuable resources for early childhood professionals. Families are essential sources of knowledge about their child's development, learning styles, strengths and challenges, and educational past. Families are also the caretakers of the child's developmental and educational future. Your professional role requires making sure that communication about children's development and learning occurs in an ongoing, reciprocal fashion. You can do this by regularly seeking family input and by contributing your own perspective. Working together, you and the family will create a shared, growing, deep understanding of their child.

SUPPORTING FAMILIES FOLLOWING DIAGNOSIS

How do you support a family after they receive a diagnosis of a delay or disability by a medical professional? Families might respond to a child's initial diagnosis in a variety of ways. Family responses are often cyclical in nature, based on their and their child's changing needs.

Family reaction and adjustment to a child's diagnosis is shaped by a variety of different factors—the child's age, the severity of disability, and any ongoing medical issues (Turnbull et al., 2005). Keep in mind that how a family responds is highly individualized. Therefore, the supports you provide them must be based on their individual needs. Families might need different kinds of supports at different times. One family might need more information, while another may need time and space to process the diagnosis. After a bit of time, the family who initially needed information might then need the space to process the diagnosis, while the family who initially needed time and space may be ready for information.

The culture of early childhood education has shaped teacher knowledge of the benefits of early intervention. Families, on the other hand, may not have an understanding of what early intervention is or how it can help. When deciding how to best support families, understand your own schemas and how these influence your perceptions and, potentially, your interactions with the families. Think carefully about a family's strengths, priorities, and concerns, and be sure to look beyond your assumptions about their reactions. Active listening is a critical component in learning more about the family's point of view. Be sure that you develop a relationship with the family that is respectful, reciprocal, and responsive to the family's needs. Some families might need resources, some further documentation, some time, some emotional support, and some confidence. All families need to know that you are responsive to their child's needs and are supportive of them in their journey.

Family knowledge and perspectives are also rich resources for the classroom. Including families in classroom activities is a great way to give them opportunities to share their knowledge and experiences. Design opportunities based on family time and comfort levels, and be sure to include appropriate amounts of coaching so family members will know what is expected and how to help. Consider offering flexible options of tasks that can be done at home, on-site in the break room, or in the classroom. Encourage families to partner with other families to complete these tasks.

Make sure volunteers understand how to help. For example, if you ask a family member to come in and read to children in her home language, try to anticipate all the questions he might have: How many children will I be reading to? What will I be reading? How long will I be reading? What if I am not comfortable reading in a group? The more explicit you can be and the more open you are to his questions, the easier it will be for a volunteer to feel comfortable participating.

Consider addressing family levels of confidence by scaffolding opportunities. Family members who are not comfortable reading to or sharing a cultural tradition with a group of young children may be happy to help with snack or play in the outdoor area. Rather than assume, work with families to match their strengths and comfort levels with meaningful ways they can participate in your setting. Listen carefully to family preferences and adapt plans as needed.

The Diallo family is involved in their daughters' classrooms in many different ways. Mr. Diallo has come in to read to both girls' classes in French, and their grandmother comes in once a week to pour juice during morning snack. The teachers have asked the family to record themselves reading to the children in French (and have provided the tape recorder) so that they can play these tapes to the accompanying books within the classroom. Whenever possible, Mrs. Diallo attends Solange's therapy sessions in the classroom and demonstrates to the teachers what she is learning from the therapies Solange has participated in at home. The family feels connected to the girls' preschool and welcomes the opportunities to participate in the classroom activities.

Chapter Reflection Questions

What are some advantages of implementing home visits within your early childhood program? What would you hope to learn from home visits?

What opportunities for family input exist within your early childhood program?

What messages does your early childhood environment convey to families? What changes do you feel you could make to create a respectful, welcoming environment that honors families?

How are Universal Design principles supported within your environment?

How might you strengthen the connection between home and the classroom environment?

What strategies do you currently use to cultivate families as resources within your early childhood program?

Questions to Explore with Families

In what ways would you like to give input into the early childhood program?

What messages do you feel are conveyed by your child's classroom environment? Do you feel welcomed, respected, and honored? What makes you feel that way? If you don't feel that way, what changes would support those feelings?

What kinds of connections would you like to build between your home and the early childhood program?

How would you like to be used as a resource within your child's early childhood program?

Appendix

Use the following factors to help you look at your program or classroom and examine your strengths and challenges. For each factor listed, indicate whether you are developing the skill or have mastered it. Next, identify what you perceive to be your strengths or challenges and any goals you have for that factor.

Family Engagement Strategies

1. Your program works to cultivate shared responsibility among the community, families, teachers, and the organization to support each child's success.
   - ◯ Developing ◯ Mastered

2. You work to reinforce learning across the multiple contexts of children's lives: home, community, school, and family.
   - ◯ Developing ◯ Mastered

3. You support the role of the family in meaningful decision-making opportunities in all aspects of their child's education.
   - ◯ Developing ◯ Mastered

4. You support the family's active participation in all aspects of their child's education.
   - ◯ Developing ◯ Mastered

5. You provide opportunities for families to share their unique knowledge through meaningful participation in events and activities.
   - ◯ Developing ◯ Mastered

6. Your program actively seeks information about each family's life and community.
   - ◯ Developing ◯ Mastered

7. Teachers integrate information about each family's life and community into the curriculum and instructional practices in a meaningful way.
   - ◯ Developing ◯ Mastered

8. Your program facilitates consistent, two-way communication that is respectful of each family's linguistic preferences.

   ○ Developing   ○ Mastered

9. Your staff takes time to learn about each family's approach to problem solving and their hopes and plans for their children.

   ○ Developing   ○ Mastered

10. Your program creates meaningful goals for children that reflect family strengths, concerns, and priorities.

    ○ Developing   ○ Mastered

11. Your program supports the staff in implementing family engagement strategies in a comprehensive and systematic way.

    ○ Developing   ○ Mastered

12. Staff strives to understand overt aspects of each family's culture, including where and how people live, style of dress, food preferences, and speech patterns.

    ○ Developing   ○ Mastered

13. Staff strives to understand deeper, covert aspects of each family's culture, including their perspectives on status (how the role of the teacher is viewed, for example, or how the family members view their role as parent within the early childhood community) or communication styles (such as preferences for greetings, eye contact, or body posture).

    ○ Developing   ○ Mastered

14. Staff strives to understand subtle aspects of each family's culture, including recognizing the embedded values and beliefs that underlie their actions (such as parenting values and how these shape goals for children's behavior).

    ○ Developing   ○ Mastered

Communication and Collaboration Skills

1. You take time to reflect on daily communication—what has gone well and what can be improved.

   ○ Developing   ○ Mastered

2. When you communicate with others, you are fully present in the exchange, thinking about what is currently happening. You attend to what the other person is saying and recognize that the outcome of the exchange will be affected by how tuned-in you are to the other person.

   ○ Developing   ○ Mastered

3. You stop and think when you respond to situations, carefully reflecting on your emotions and underlying schemas.

   ○ Developing   ○ Mastered

4. You are aware of the NAEYC *Code of Ethical Conduct* and use it to guide your interactions with families.

   ○ Developing   ○ Mastered

5. You demonstrate your interest in a speaker by leaning in slightly, having open arms, and nodding your head.

   ○ Developing   ○ Mastered

6. You verbally reflect messages you hear from the speaker and communicate interest by using comments.

   ○ Developing   ○ Mastered

7. You use questions to make sure you clearly understand the speaker's point of view.

   ○ Developing   ○ Mastered

8. You restate messages to make sure that your understanding is correct.

   ○ Developing   ○ Mastered

9. At the end of a conversation, you review major highlights of what has been discussed.

   ○ Developing   ○ Mastered

10. You add your own ideas to those of the speaker. You provide specific knowledge and information based on the needs of the speaker.
    ○ Developing   ○ Mastered

11. You work to create consensus by reaching agreed-upon goals.
    ○ Developing   ○ Mastered

12. In the face of conflict, you mindfully communicate and work to understand your own schemas.
    ○ Developing   ○ Mastered

13. In the face of conflict, you actively listen and establish reciprocity with the other person. You work to establish a third space.
    ○ Developing   ○ Mastered

Understanding Social Identities and Cultural Frameworks

1. You strive to identify your own personal identities and cultural frameworks and the ways these may influence relationships with families.
   - ○ Developing   ○ Mastered

2. Staff strives to identify the cultural scripts that guide their expectations for children's development and learning.
   - ○ Developing   ○ Mastered

3. Staff strives to learn about cultural scripts that guide family choices and behavior, including hopes and dreams for their child, what their child's behavior means to the family, the family's goals for their child's behavior, and the family's goals for the child as an adult.
   - ○ Developing   ○ Mastered

4. You use open-ended questions to learn about families' meaningful cultural practices.
   - ○ Developing   ○ Mastered

5. You use open-ended questions to learn if and how families would like their cultural practices included in the early childhood environment.
   - ○ Developing   ○ Mastered

6. You use open-ended questions to learn about a family's goals for their child's development.
   - ○ Developing   ○ Mastered

7. The staff reflects the understanding that home and program rules may differ and that careful communication must address and respect these differences.
   - ○ Developing   ○ Mastered

8. The staff is careful to learn about and respect subtle cultural rules.
   - ○ Developing   ○ Mastered

9. The staff observes to learn who makes the decisions in a family.
   - ○ Developing   ○ Mastered

10. The staff is responsive to and respectful of family communication patterns.

   ○ Developing   ○ Mastered

11. The staff offers families opportunities to discuss child-rearing beliefs.

   ○ Developing   ○ Mastered

Developing Culturally Competent Communication

1. Staff carefully considers nonverbal communication and strives to create continuity with families in the choice and degree of self-disclosure, permission of touch, boundaries of personal space, use of gestures, use of facial expressions, use of eye contact, and preferred greetings.
   - ○ Developing   ○ Mastered

2. The program determines each family's primary language and dialect and secures an interpreter, if needed.
   - ○ Developing   ○ Mastered

3. The staff connects with family stories.
   - ○ Developing   ○ Mastered

4. The staff shows respect, acknowledges values, and is open to the process of communication.
   - ○ Developing   ○ Mastered

5. You gather information about a family's cultural history, including their beliefs and values, their living situation, their family structure, their language and literacy, their community affiliations, their network of social support, their challenges, and their economic situation.
   - ○ Developing   ○ Mastered

6. You use appropriate skills in interacting with families, including establishing rapport, demonstrating empathy, providing support, developing a partnership, providing explanations, demonstrating cultural competence, and developing trust.
   - ○ Developing   ○ Mastered

Culturally and Linguistically Competent Organizations

1. Families have meaningful input into all aspects of program planning and decision making, including curriculum, finance, and opportunities to serve as board members.
   ○ Developing   ○ Mastered

2. The program provides financial supports for needed professional development.
   ○ Developing   ○ Mastered

3. Child care, meals, and transportation are provided to encourage family participation in events and meetings.
   ○ Developing   ○ Mastered

4. Program policies and practices support hiring staff who speak the home languages of the children in the classrooms.
   ○ Developing   ○ Mastered

5. The program strives to hire staff who mirror community demographics.
   ○ Developing   ○ Mastered

6. The program provides family education activities to support their understanding of educational theory and developmentally appropriate classroom practices.
   ○ Developing   ○ Mastered

7. Families receive an orientation to the program designed to ensure that they understand how to meaningfully engage with the program.
   ○ Developing   ○ Mastered

8. The program strives to communicate to families the positive outcomes of family engagement and how much the program values their input.
   ○ Developing   ○ Mastered

9. Families are invited to staff development workshops.
   ○ Developing   ○ Mastered

10. Families have opportunities to offer input on workshop topics.
○ Developing ○ Mastered

11. Families are surveyed about events and activities and have opportunities to participate in event planning.
○ Developing ○ Mastered

12. Families are surveyed about building use and ideas for change.
○ Developing ○ Mastered

13. Families are educated about their rights and role in their child's education, including information about identification, referral, and intervention processes and legal, ethical, and financial matters.
○ Developing ○ Mastered

14. Families and staff receive information on their roles in the development and implementation of ISFPs and IEPs.
○ Developing ○ Mastered

15. Staff meeting time is dedicated to exploring cross-cultural issues.
○ Developing ○ Mastered

16. Staff receives training on communicating with diverse families, including the topics of translations, interpreters, cultural mediators, and understanding cultural practices.
○ Developing ○ Mastered

17. Staff receives training on local cultures and culturally based definitions of child development and early childhood education.
○ Developing ○ Mastered

18. Staff receives training on how culture influences their own practices and beliefs.
○ Developing ○ Mastered

19. Staff receives training on culturally competent communication practices.
○ Developing ○ Mastered

20. When necessary, translators are provided for family conferences and general communication.
    ○ Developing   ○ Mastered

21. During conferences, families and staff discuss understandings of child goals, strengths, and challenges. The staff uses this information to establish a shared framework of learning goals for children.
    ○ Developing   ○ Mastered

22. Program communications are translated into the home languages of the families served.
    ○ Developing   ○ Mastered

23. Program communications are distributed in a variety formats to increase accessibility.
    ○ Developing   ○ Mastered

24. The program regularly assesses family satisfaction with communication methods.
    ○ Developing   ○ Mastered

25. The program uses family surveys to individualize communications based on family preferences.
    ○ Developing   ○ Mastered

26. The program provides opportunities for community members to serve on advisory boards and committees.
    ○ Developing   ○ Mastered

27. Program practices complement and support the needs of the community.
    ○ Developing   ○ Mastered

28. Program policies are informed by the histories and traditions of the families served.
    ○ Developing   ○ Mastered

Culturally and Linguistically Competent Classrooms

1. Teachers plan home visits carefully, with extensive thought given to the purpose of the visit and up-front communication with the family.
   - ○ Developing   ○ Mastered

2. For home visits, teachers plan greetings, activities, and information to share.
   - ○ Developing   ○ Mastered

3. Teachers listen to family stories and use them to learn about each family's cultural framework and communication style.
   - ○ Developing   ○ Mastered

4. After home visits, teachers follow up with the family.
   - ○ Developing   ○ Mastered

5. Families are aware of what is happening in the classroom.
   - ○ Developing   ○ Mastered

6. Families have opportunities to offer input on the curriculum.
   - ○ Developing   ○ Mastered

7. Staff regularly surveys families about the effects of classroom policies and ideas for change.
   - ○ Developing   ○ Mastered

8. Staff strives to avoid jargon when communicating with families.
   - ○ Developing   ○ Mastered

9. Teachers strive to address any obstacles to family involvement, including lack of transportation, lack of child care, distrust of institutions, and unclear expectations.
   - ○ Developing   ○ Mastered

10. Families' authentic social identities are represented in the early childhood environment.
    ○ Developing   ○ Mastered

11. The design of the environment takes into account each family's language, culture, and unique abilities.
    ○ Developing   ○ Mastered

12. Materials are translated into families' home languages and take into account the literacy levels of the families served.
    ○ Developing   ○ Mastered

13. Families have space in the environment for one-on-one conversations, private conferences, and conversations with other families.
    ○ Developing   ○ Mastered

14. The environment is equally appealing to all participants.
    ○ Developing   ○ Mastered

15. The pictures posted within the environment reflect the homes, communities, and abilities of the children and families served.
    ○ Developing   ○ Mastered

16. Information is shared in a variety of different formats, including face-to-face conversations, video, online, written, and pictorial.
    ○ Developing   ○ Mastered

17. Information is presented in the families' home languages.
    ○ Developing   ○ Mastered

18. Information about where things are located, how to access materials, how to use the space, and where to go if experiencing challenges is posted in languages reflected in the environment and takes into account different literacy levels.
    ○ Developing   ○ Mastered

19. Families can enter the classroom environment and immediately know or intuit expectations.

    ◯ Developing   ◯ Mastered

20. Families understand expectations at drop-off and pickup times, and the environment supports success.

    ◯ Developing   ◯ Mastered

21. There are comfortable places for families to communicate with other families or with teaching staff and for families to spend time with children during daily transitions.

    ◯ Developing   ◯ Mastered

22. Furnishings and accessories mirror the present family population and are adjusted accordingly over time.

    ◯ Developing   ◯ Mastered

23. Staff routinely asks families for their input on policies and procedures.

    ◯ Developing   ◯ Mastered

24. Families have many opportunities to offer information about their children's strengths and concerns.

    ◯ Developing   ◯ Mastered

25. Staff routinely asks families about their priorities for their children.

    ◯ Developing   ◯ Mastered

26. Teachers offer a wide variety of home extension activities, taking into account families' time constraints and comfort levels.

    ◯ Developing   ◯ Mastered

27. Teachers provide information on the purpose of the activities and instructions on how to successfully implement the activities.

    ◯ Developing   ◯ Mastered

References and Recommended Reading

Albert, Saul, and David Whetten. 1985. "Organizational Identity." *Research in Organizational Behavior* 7: 263–295.

Al-Hassan, Suha, and Ralph Gardner. 2002. "Involving Immigrant Parents of Students with Disabilities in the Educational Process." *Teaching Exceptional Children* 34: 52–58.

Annie E. Casey Foundation. 2006. *Race Matters: Unequal Opportunities for School Readiness*. Baltimore, MD: Annie E. Casey Foundation. www.aecf.org/upload/publicationfiles/fact_sheet2.pdf

Barrera, Isaura, and Robert Corso. 2002. "Cultural Competency as Skilled Dialogue." *Topics in Early Childhood Special Education* 22(2): 103–113.

Barrera, Isaura, Robert Corso, and Dianne Macpherson. 2003. *Skilled Dialogue: Strategies for Responding to Cultural Diversity in Early Childhood*. Baltimore, MD: Paul H. Brookes.

Bennett, Tess, et al. 2001. Cross-Cultural Considerations in Early Childhood Special Education, *Technical Report No. 14*. Culturally and Linguistically Appropriate Services. http://clas.uiuc.edu/techreport/tech14.html

Borden, George. 1991. *Cultural Orientation: An Approach to Understanding Intercultural Communication*. Englewood Cliffs, NJ: Prentice Hall.

Brorson, Kent. 2005. "The Culture of a Home Visit in Early Intervention." *Journal of Early Childhood Research* 3(1): 51–76.

Brown, Kirk, and Richard Ryan. 2003. "The Benefits of Being Present: Mindfulness and Its Role in Psychological Well-Being." *Journal of Personality and Social Psychology* 84(4): 822–848.

Buysse, Virginia, Barbara Goldman, and Martie Skinner. 2002. "Setting Effects on Friendship Formation among Young Children with and without Disabilities." *Exceptional Children* 68(4): 503–517.

Buysse, Virginia, and Patricia Wesley. 2006. "Evidence-Based Practice: How Did It Emerge and What Does It Really Mean for the Early Childhood Field?" In *Evidence-Based Practice in the Early Childhood Field*. Washington, DC: Zero to Three.

Carlisle, Erin, Lindsey Stanley, and Kristen Kemple. 2005. "Opening Doors: Understanding School and Family Influences on Family Involvement." *Early Childhood Educational Journal* 33(3): 155–162.

Children's Defense Fund. 2012. *Portrait of Inequality: Black Children in America*. Washington, DC: Children's Defense Fund. www.childrensdefense.org/child-research-data-publications/data/portrait-of-inequality-2011.html

ChildStats. 2012. America's Children in Brief: Key Indicators of Well-Being, 2012. ChildStats.gov. www.childstats.gov/americaschildren/famsoc.asp

Child Trends and SRI International. 2002. *First Five California: Child, Family, and Community Indicators Book*. Sacramento, CA: California Children and Families Commission. www.ccfc.ca.gov/pdf/research/reference/Child_Family_and_Community_Indicators.pdf

Christian, Linda. 2006. "Understanding Families: Applying Family Systems Theory to Early Childhood Practice." *Young Children* 61(1): 12–20.

Cohn, D'Vera, and Tara Bahrampour. 2006. "Of U.S. Children Under 5, Nearly Half Are Minorities." *The Washington Post*, May 10.

Constantino, Steven. 2008. *101 Ways to Create Real Family Engagement*. Galax, VA: Engage Press.

Cross, Terry, et al. 1989. *Towards a Culturally Competent System of Care: A Monograph on Effective Service for Minority Children Who Are Severely Emotionally Disturbed.* Washington, DC: Georgetown University Child Development Center, CASSP Technical Assistance Center. www.mhsoac.ca.gov/meetings/docs/Meetings/2010/June/CLCC_Tab_4_Towards_Culturally_Competent_System.pdf

Deaux, Kay. 2001. "Social Identity." In *Encyclopedia of Women and Gender.* Maryland Heights, MO: Academic Press.

DEC/NAEYC. 2009. *Early Childhood Inclusion: A Joint Position Statement of the Division for Early Childhood (DEC) and the National Association for the Education of Young Children (NAEYC).* Chapel Hill: The University of North Carolina, FPG Child Development Institute.

Ekman, Paul. 2007. *Emotions Revealed: Recognizing Faces and Feelings to Improve Communication and Emotional Life.* New York: Holt.

Englund, Michelle, Byron Englund, and Andrew Collins. 2008. "Exceptions to High School Drop Out Predictions in a Low-Income Sample: Do Adults Make a Difference?" *Journal of Social Issues* 64(1): 77–93.

Farkas, George. 2003. "Cognitive Skills and Noncognitive Traits and Behaviors in Stratification Processes." *Annual Review of Sociology* 29: 541–562.

Flores, Glenn, Sandra Tomany-Korman, and Lynn Olson. 2005. "Does Disadvantage Start at Home? Racial and Ethnic Disparities in Health-Related Early Childhood Home Routines and Safety Practices." *Archives of Pediatrics and Adolescent Medicine* 159(2): 158–165.

Frey, William. 2011. "America Reaches Its Demographic Tipping Point." *Up Front.* http://www.brookings.edu/blogs/up-front/posts/2011/08/26-census-race-frey

Garcia Winner, Michelle, and Pamela Crooke. 2011. *Socially Curious and Curiously Social: A Social Thinking Guidebook for Bright Teens and Young Adults.* San Jose, CA: Think Social Publishing.

Gardenswartz, Lee, and Anita Rowe. 1998. *Managing Diversity in Health Care.* San Francisco: Jossey-Bass.

Gilbert, Jean, Tawara Goode, and Clara Dunne. 2007. *Cultural Awareness.* Washington, DC: National Center for Cultural Competence, Georgetown University Center for Child and Human Development.

Ginsberg, Margery. 2007. "Lessons at the Kitchen Table." *Educational Leadership* 64(6): 6–61.

Golden, Olivia. 2011. *Head Start and the Changing Demographics of Today's Young Children.* National Head Start Association Dialog Brief. www.urban.org/uploadedpdf/109046-head-start-changing-demographics-todays-children.pdf

González, Norma, Luis Moll, and Cathy Amanti. 2005. *Funds of Knowledge: Theorizing Practices in Households, Communities, and Classrooms.* Mahway, NJ: Lawrence Erlbaum.

Goode, Tawara, and Wendy Jones. 2009. *Definition of Linguistic Competence.* National Center for Cultural Competence. Washington, DC: Georgetown University Center for Child and Human Development. http://nccc.georgetown.edu/resources/Dental_Initiative2.html

Gorski, Paul. 2007. "The Question of Class." *Teaching Tolerance* 31(Spring). http://www.tolerance.org/magazine/number-31-spring-2007/feature/question-class

Halgunseth, Linda, et al. 2009. *Family Engagement, Diverse Families, and Early Childhood Education Programs: An Integrated Review of the Literature.* Washington, DC: NAEYC.

Harris, Scott. 2008. "What is Family Diversity? Objective and Interpretive Approaches." *Journal of Family Issues* 29(11): 1407–1417.

Harvard Family Research Project. 2006. *Family Involvement Makes a Difference: Evidence that Family Involvement Promotes School Success for Every Child of Every Age.* Cambridge, MA: Harvard Family Research Project: Harvard Graduate School of Education.

Henderson, Anne, and Karen Mapp. 2002. *A New Wave of Evidence: The Impact of School, Family, and Community Connections on Student Achievement.* Austin, TX: Southwest Educational Development Laboratory.

Hepburn, Kathy. 2004. *Families as Primary Partners in Their Child's Development and School Readiness.* Baltimore, MD: Annie E. Casey Foundation. www.aecf.org/upload/publicationfiles/families.pdf

Hernandez, Donald, Nancy Denton, and Suzanne McCartney. 2007. *Children in Immigrant Families—The U.S. and 50 States: National Origins, Language, and Early Education. Child Trends and the Center for Social and Demographic Analysis.* Albany, NY: University at Albany, SUNY. http://www.childtrends.org/wp-content/uploads/2013/04/child_trends-2007_04_01_rb_childrenimmigrant.pdf

Howe, Laura. 1972. *The Future of the Family.* New York: Simon and Schuster.

Hunt, Pam, et al. 2004. "Collaborative Teaming to Support Preschoolers with Severe Disabilities Who Are Placed in General Education Early Childhood Programs." Topics in *Early Childhood Special Education* 24(3): 123–142.

Huston, Dan. 2010. *Communicating Mindfully: Mindfulness-Based Communication and Emotional Intelligence. Independence,* KY: Cengage Learning.

Izzo, Charles, Roger Weissberg, Wesley Kasprow, and Michael Fendrich. 1999. "A Longitudinal Assessment of Teacher Perceptions of Parent Involvement in Children's Education and School Performance." *American Journal of Community Psychology* 27(6): 817–839.

Jezewski, Mary Ann. 1990. "Culture Brokering in Migrant Farm Worker Health Care." *Western Journal of Nursing Research* 12(4): 497–513.

Kalyanpur, Maya, and Beth Harry. 2012. *Cultural Reciprocity in Special Education.* Baltimore, MD: Paul H. Brookes.

Kalyanpur, Maya, Beth Harry, and Tom Skrtic. 2000. "Equity and Advocacy Expectations of Culturally Diverse Families' Participation in Special Education." *International Journal of Disability, Development and Education* 47(2): 119–136.

Kaser, Sandy, and Kathy Short. 1998. "Exploring Culture through Children's Connections." *Language Arts* 75(3): 185–192.

Kidd, Julia, Sylvia Sánchez, and Eva Thorp. 2002. "A Focus on Family Stories: Enhancing Preservice Teachers' Cultural Awareness." In *Fifty-First Yearbook of the National Reading Conference.* Chicago: National Reading Conference.

Kids Count. 2012. "Children Living in America's High-Poverty Communities." *Data Snapshot on High-Poverty Communities.* Baltimore, MD: Annie E. Casey Foundation. www.aecf.org/~/media/Pubs/Initiatives/KIDS%20COUNT/D/DataSnapshotonHighPovertyCommunities/KIDSCOUNTDataSnapshot_HighPovertyCommunities.pdf.

Kuhl, Patricia. 2004. "Early Language Acquisition: Cracking the Speech Code." *Nature Reviews Neuroscience* 5(11): 831–843.

Lareau, Annette. 1989. *Home Advantage: Social Class and Parental Intervention in Elementary Education.* New York: Falmer Press.

Leichter, Hope. 1996. "Creative Intelligence of Families: Bridges to School Learning." *Equity and Excellence in Education* 29(1): 77–85.

Long, Carol. 2011. "Ten Best Practices to Enhance Culturally Competent Communication in Palliative Care." *Journal of Pediatric Oncology* 33(2): 136–139.

Lynch, Eleanor, and Marci Hanson. 2004. "Family Diversity, Assessment, and Cultural Competence." In *Assessing Infants and Preschoolers with Special Needs,* 3rd ed. Columbus, OH: Merrill.

Mantizicopoulos, Panayota. 2003. "Flunking Kindergarten after Head Start: An Inquiry into the Contribution of Contextual and Individual Variables." *Journal of Educational Psychology* 95(2): 268–278.

Maschinot, Beth. 2008. *The Changing Face of the United States: The Influence of Culture on Child Development.* Washington, DC: Zero to Three.

Mathematica Policy Research. 2012. *Supporting Evidence-Based Home Visiting to Prevent Child Maltreatment.* www.mathematica-mpr.com/earlychildhood/evidencebasedhomevisiting.asp

Matthews, Hannah, and Deanna Jang. 2007. *The Challenges of Change: Learning from the Child Care and Early Education Experiences of Immigrant Families.* Washington, DC: Center for Law and Social Policy. http://www.clasp.org/resources-and-publications/files/0356.pdf

McWayne, Christine, et al. 2004. "A Multivariate Examination of Parent Involvement and the Social and Academic Competencies of Urban Kindergarten Children." *Psychology in the Schools* 41(3): 363–377.

McWayne, Christine, and Marissa Owsianik. 2004. "Parent Involvement and the Social and Academic Competencies of Urban Kindergarten Children." *Family Involvement Research Digests*. Cambridge, MA: Harvard Family Research Project. http://www.hfrp.org/publications-resources/publications-series/family-involvement-research-digests/parent-involvement-and-the-social-and-academic-competencies-of-urban-kindergarten-children

Mechelli, Andrea, et al. 2011. "Neurolinguistics: Structural Plasticity in the Bilingual Brain." *Nature* 431: 757.

Mutha, Sunita, Carol Allen, and Melissa Welch. 2002. *Toward Culturally Competent Care: A Toolbox for Teaching Communication Strategies*. San Francisco, CA: Center for the Health Professions.

National Association for the Education of Young Children. 2005. *Code of Ethical Conduct and Statement of Commitment*. Washington, DC: NAEYC. www.naeyc.org/files/naeyc/file/positions/PSETH05.pdf

National Association for the Education of Young Children. 2009. *Quality Benchmark for Cultural Competence Project*. Washington, DC: NAEYC. www.naeyc.org/files/naeyc/file/policy/state/QBCC_Tool.pdf

National Center for Children in Poverty. 2012. "Child Poverty." New York: Mailman School of Public Health, Columbia University. www.nccp.org/topics/childpoverty.html

National Center for Cultural Competence. 2006. "Cultural and Linguistic Competence Policy Assessment." Washington, DC: Georgetown University Center for Child and Human Development, University Center for Excellence in Developmental Disabilities. www.clcpa.info/documents/CLCPA.pdf

National Center for Cultural Competence. n.d. "Process of Inquiry: Communicating in a Multicultural Environment." Curricula Enhancement Module Series. Washington, DC: Georgetown University Center for Child and Human Development. www.ncccurricula.info/communication/index.html

National Center for Cultural Competence. n.d. "Working with Linguistically Diverse Populations." Washington, DC: Georgetown University Center for Child and Human Development http://nccc.georgetown.edu/features/language.html

Ngo, Bic. 2008. "Beyond 'Culture Clash': Understanding of Immigrant Experiences." *Theory into Practice* 47(1): 4–11.

Nieto, Leticia, and Margot Boyer. 2010. *Beyond Inclusion, Beyond Empowerment: A Developmental Strategy to Liberate Everyone*. Lacey, WA: Cuetzpalin.

Nissen, Laura. 2001. *Strengths-Based Approaches to Work with Youth and Families: An Overview of the Literature and Web-based Resources*. http://www.npcresearch.com/Files/YCA/Strengths_based_Approaches_Nissen_2001.pdf

Odom, Samuel, ed. 2002. *Widening the Circle: Including Children with Disabilities in Preschool Programs*. New York: Teachers College Press.

Office of Head Start. 2008. *Dual Language Learning: What Does It Take?* Washington, DC: Administration for Children and Families, U.S. Department of Health and Human Services.

Office of Head Start. 2011. *The Head Start Parent, Family, and Community Engagement Framework: Promoting Family Engagement and School Readiness from Prenatal to Age 8*. Arlington, VA: Administration for Children and Families, U.S. Department of Health and Human Services. http://eclkc.ohs.acf.hhs.gov/hslc/standards/ims/2011/pfce-framework.pdf

O'Hair, Dan, and Mary Wiemann. 2011. *Real Communication: An Introduction*. New York: Bedford/St. Martin's.

Olds, Anita. 2001. *Child Care Design Guide*. New York: McGraw Hill.

Price-Robertson, Rhys. 2010. *Supporting Young Parents*. CAFCA Practice Sheet. Melbourne, VIC: Australian Institute of Family Studies. http://www.aifs.gov.au/cafca/pubs/sheets/ps/ps3.pdf

Puig, Victoria. 2010. "Are Early Intervention Services Placing Home Languages and Cultures 'At Risk'?" *Early Childhood Research and Practice* 12(2). http://ecrp.uiuc.edu/v12n1/puig.html.

Ramsey, Patricia. 2004. *Teaching and Learning in a Diverse World: Multicultural Education for Young Children*, 3rd ed. New York: Teachers College Press.

Rosenthal, Miriam, and Dorit Roer-Strier. 2001. "Cultural Differences in Mothers' Developmental Goals and Ethnotheories." *International Journal of Psychology* 36(1): 20–31.

Saint-Jacques, Marie-Christine, Daniel Turcotte, and Eve Pouliot. 2009. "Adopting a Strengths Perspective in Social Work Practice with Families in Difficulty: From Theory to Practice." *Families in Society* 90(4): 454–461.

Sánchez, Sylvia. 1999. "Learning from the Stories of Culturally and Linguistically Diverse Families and Communities." *Remedial and Special Education* 20(6): 351–359.

Seeye, Ned, and Jacqueline Wasilewski. 1996. *Between Cultures: Developing Self-Identity in a World of Diversity.* Lincolnwood, IL: McGraw-Hill.

Solomon, Andrew. 2012. *Far from the Tree: Families, Children, and the Search for Identity.* New York: Simon and Schuster.

Soto, Lourdes. 1991. "Understanding Bilingual/Bicultural Young Children." *Young Children* 46(2): 30–36.

Speilberg, Lela. 2011. "Successful Family Engagement in the Classroom: What Teachers Need to Know and Be Able to Do to Engage Families in Raising Student Achievement." *FINE: Family Involvement Network of Educators Newsletter* 3(1). http://www.hfrp.org/var/hfrp/storage/fckeditor/File/file/FINE%20Newsletter/Winter2011/FINE-Flamboyan_Article.pdf

Stark, Deborah. 2010. *Engaged Families, Effective Pre-K: State Policies that Bolster Student Success.* Washington, DC: The PEW Center on the States. www.pewtrusts.org/uploadedFiles/wwwpewtrustsorg/Reports/Pre-k_education/PkN_Family_Engagement_FINAL.pdf

Steinfeld, Edward, and Jordana Maisel. 2012. *Universal Design: Creating Inclusive Environments.* Hoboken, NJ: John Wiley and Sons.

Surbone, Antonella, and Walter Baile. 2010. *Pocket Guide of Culturally Competent Communication.* Austin, TX: University of Texas MD Anderson Cancer Center. www.mdanderson.org/education-and-research/resources-for-professionals/professional-educational-resources/i-care/ICAREguide_CultComp.pdf

Technical Assistance and Training System. 2009. *Families and Their Children with Disabilities—Grieving or Dealing with Acceptance?* www.tats.ucf.edu/docs/eupdates/FamilyInvolvement-8.pdf

Thomas, Carol, Vivian Correa, and Catherine Morsink. 2000. *Interactive Teaming,* 3rd ed. Upper Saddle River, NJ: Prentice Hall/Merrill.

Thorp, Eva. 1997. "Increasing Opportunities for Partnership with Culturally and Linguistically Diverse Families." *Intervention in School and Clinic* 32(5): 261–269.

Tienda, Marta, and Ron Haskins. 2011. "Immigrant Children: Introducing the Issue." *The Future of Children* 21(1): 3–18.

Turnbull, Ann, and John Summers. 1987. "From Parent Involvement to Family Support: Evolution to Revolution." In *New Perspectives on Down Syndrome: Proceedings of the State-of-the-Art Conference.* Baltimore, MD: Paul H. Brookes.

Turnbull, Ann, et al. 2005. *Families, Professionals, and Exceptionality: Positive Outcomes Through Partnership and Trust,* 5th ed. Upper Saddle River, NJ: Pearson Merrill Prentice Hall.

U.S. Census Bureau. 2010. *United States Census 2010.* www.census.gov/2010census

U.S. Department of Education. 2010. *29th Annual Report to Congress on the Implementation of the Individuals with Disabilities Education Act, 2007, vol. 1.* Washington, DC: Office of Special Education and Rehabilitative Services, Office of Special Education Programs.

Valdés, Guadalupe. 1996. *Con Respeto—Bridging the Distances between Culturally Diverse Families and Schools.* New York: Teachers College Press.

Wang, Jianglong. 2011. "Communication and Cultural Competence: The Acquisition of Cultural Knowledge and Behavior." *Online Readings in Psychology and Culture* 7(1). http://scholarworks.gvsu.edu/orpc/vol7/iss1/3

Weiss, Heather, and Elena Lopez. 2009. "Redefining Family Engagement in Education." *FINE Family Involvement Network Newsletter* 2(1). www.hfrp.org/family-involvement/publications-resources/redefining-family-engagement-in-education

Weiss, Heather, Elena Lopez, and Heidi Rosenberg. 2010. "Beyond Random Acts: Family, School, and Community Engagement as an Integral Part of Education Reform." Cambridge, MA: Harvard Family Research Project. www.hfrp.org/publications-resources/browse-our-publications/beyond-random-acts-family-school-and-community-engagement-as-an-integral-part-of-education-reform

Winton, Pam, et al. 2010. "Module 3: Communication for Collaboration." Connect Modules. Chapel Hill: University of North Carolina, FPG Child Development Institute, Connect: The Center to Mobilize Early Childhood Knowledge. http://community.fpg.unc.edu/connect-modules/learners/module-3

Winton, Pam, and Jeanette McCollum. 2008. "Preparing and Supporting High-Quality Early Childhood Practitioners: Issues and evidence." In *Preparing and Supporting Effective Practitioners: Evidence and Applications in Early Childhood and Early Intervention.* Washington, DC: Zero to Three.

Index